AT HIS SIDE

THE LAST YEARS OF ISAAC BABEL

❋

A. N. Pirozhkova

Translated by Anne Frydman & Robert L. Busch

STEERFORTH PRESS

South Royalton, Vermont

For information about permission to reproduce selections
from this book, write to: Steerforth Press L.C., P.O. Box 70,
South Royalton, Vermont 05068.

ACKNOWLEDGMENTS
Grateful acknowledgment is made to the Canadian Slavonic
Papers/Revue *canadienne des slavisles* in which A. N. Pirozhkova's
memoir was first published in English in a slightly different version
[Vol. XXXVI, Nos. 1–2, March–June, 1944].

The author expresses her gratitude to her grandson, Andrei Malaev-
Babel, and his wife, Lisa Eveland Malaev, for their invaluable help in
preparing this book for publication.

Anne Frydman wishes to thank the International Research and
Exchanges Board and the U.S. State Department (Title VII program)
for their support in her research for this work.

Library of Congress Cataloging-in-Publication Data
Pirozhkova, A. N. (Antonina Nikolaevna)
At his side : the last years of Isaac Babel / A. N. Pirozhkova ;
translated by Anne Frydman and Robert L. Busch. — 1st ed.
p. cm.
ISBN 1-883642-37-X (alk. paper)
1. Babel, I. (Isaak), 1894–1941–Last years. 2. Pirozhkova, A. N. (Antonina
Nikolaevna). 3. Authors, Russian–20th century–Biography. 4. Authors'
spouses–Soviet Union–Biography.
I. Title.
PG3476.B2Z778 1996
891.73'42
[B] dc20   96-33283
CIP

Manufactured in the United States of America

FIRST EDITION

FOREWORD

WHEN I READ Antonina Nikolaevna Pirozhkova's memoir of daily life with Isaac Babel I realized that I'd known very little about him. Only his death was famous. And of course until fairly recently most of us had that wrong too. But I did know his work, though not until the early sixties when the Meridian edition first appeared.

One must begin by telling those who still don't know those stories that they are unusual in a particular way. That is, any one of them, those in *Red Cavalry* and *Tales of Odessa*, as well as those extracted only in the last few years from bureaus and closets of old Russian friends, can be read again and again. I don't mean every five or ten years. I mean in one evening a story you read just six months ago can be read a couple of times — and not because the story is a difficult one. There's so much plain nutrition in it, the absolute accuracy and astonishment in the language, the breadth of the body and the height of the soul.

You *do* feel yourself healthier, spiritually speaking, if also sadder — or happier, depending on the story.

Where did those sentences, that language, come from? Babel's head in childhood was buried in Hebrew, in Talmudic studies. His adolescent head was European, full of French. Russian was an everyday matter, clear and crisp, the vowels in an armor of consonants. His grandmother spoke Ukranian. When he was ten he came to Odessa. It was like every tough city, full of smart talkers; you could listen to that city all day and begin again the next. Some kind of lucky composting had begun.

It was in Odessa, on his way to becoming a real Russian, that the story "Awakening" was made. He was supposed to be taking violin lessons, which would help him become a man like Jascha Heifetz. He would then play for the Queen of England. Somehow he began to never reach his music school but wandered walking in Odessa down to the docks. He found, or was found by, a good man, the kind who appears in a child's wandering time to say, "Go this way, not that!" — forcefully. He taught the boy the names of flowers and asked, "Well, what is it you lack? A feeling for nature. What's that tree?" The boy didn't know. "That bird? That bush?" Then he said, "And you dare to call yourself a writer?" (The boy had been daring.) He would never be a writer, a *Russian* writer, without knowing the natural world. "What were your parents thinking of?" But those days were also among his first meetings with the "others" — the wild free Russian boys, diving, swimming, clambering on the boats, the ships in Odessa harbor. He is finally taught to swim. At last he can join them.

Years later, still longing, like most young Jewish revolutionaries (like my own parents) to become a real Russian, he has a harder time with the "others." The revolution has happened. The civil war is unending. Liutov (the name he gives the narrator of the Red Cavalry stories) is assigned to the Cossacks of Savitsky's VI Division. He is billeted with half a dozen other Cossacks who look at the "specks" (eyeglasses) on his nose, are disgusted, and want to look no further. The quartermaster who has delivered him says, "Nuisance with specks . . . but you go and mess up a lady, and a good lady too, and you'll have the boys patting you on the back." There are no women around but the landlady. He's hungry. He sees the goose, takes hold of it, places his heavy boot on its neck, cracks its head, presents it to the landlady. "Cook it!" "Hey you," one of the Cossacks calls out almost immediately, "Sit down and feed with us." He's asked to read them the news. Out of *Pravda* he proudly reads Lenin's speech and is happy to "spy out the secret curve of Lenin's straight line." They slept then, all with their legs intermingled. "In my dreams I saw women. But my heart, stained with bloodshed, grated and brimmed over."

Loneliness, differentness, hunger enabled him to brutally kill the goose. But he was unable to go much further. In the case of Dolgushov ("The Death of Dolgushov"), he could not bring himself to end Dolgushov's agony, though the Cossack's belly was pouring his intestines out of its wide wound and Dolgushov begs him to "waste a cartridge" on him. He cannot do it and he hears words of contempt from the comrade, Afonka, who has pity for Dolgushov and helps him to leave this life.

And later, in "Going Into Battle," caught with an unloaded pistol, he asks "for the simplest of proficiencies, the ability to kill my fellow man."

※

IN A STORY FROM *Red Cavalry,* "Sandy the Christ" (so named for his noticeable mildness) hears his stepfather in his mother's bed. He calls out to stop him, to remind his stepfather that he is "tainted." He begs him to consider his mother's fine white skin, her innocence, then trades them for permission from this man to become the village herdsman. I have read that story many times and, as I come to the last paragraphs, my heart still beats faster. Of course it isn't the story line alone, which is certainly interesting. It must be the way of telling.

How did he come to that?

When he was quite young he loved French literature, particularly Flaubert and Maupassant. In fact, according to information in *You Must Know Everything,* he wrote his first stories in French. Then he began to think about how to write about war: he came upon *Authentic Stories of the Great War* by the French writer Captain Gaston Vidal. He admired the stories, the facts of the stories. But he had just come back from fighting on the Romanian front and was soon to become Liutov, the war correspondent, the writer, the storyteller for the Red Cavalry, Budenny's First Cavalry. He began to translate the stories and in one long moment (all his writing moments were extremely long) he created a language, a style, his brand-new sentences. In *You Must Know Everything* there is an excellent example. By reducing a tendentious twelve-line paragraph from one of those stories to three lines, he produced clarity, presentness, tension, and a model of how always, though with great difficulty, to proceed.

Here is Babel talking about his method of working with Kostantin Paustovsky in his book *Years of Hope.*

"If you use enough elbow grease even the coarsest wood gets to look like ivory. That's what we have to do with words and with our Russian language. Warm it and polish it with your hand till it glows like a jewel. . . .

"The first version of a story is terrible. All in bits and pieces tied together with boring 'like passages' as dry as old rope. You have the first version of "Lyubka" there, you can see for yourself. It yaps at you. It's clumsy, helpless, toothless. That's where the real work begins. I go over each sentence time and time again. I start by cutting out all the words I can do without. Words are very sly. The rubbishy ones go into hiding . . . After that I type the story and let it lie for two or three days. Then I check it again sentence by sentence . . . I shorten the sentences and break up the paragraphs."

In the end there were twenty-two versions of "Lyubka the Cossack," a wild story full of smugglers, infants, an old man, contraband, brothels, sailors, traveling salesmen, prostitutes, a baby howling to be nursed. A short story!

To make matters clearer he wrote a story about the French writer he loved. It's called "Guy de Maupassant." In it the art of translation, the game of love, and the punctuation of sentences are of equal lively value. After years of love for this master he said one day, startled with the knowledge, "You know Maupassant — he has no heart."

In the course of Babel's long conversation with Paustovsky, he said, "I've got no imagination. All I've got is the longing for it." What could he have done with more imagination? He was a Jew, his childhood spent in the provincial ghetto of a provincial town. Only fifteen years later he became the great chronicler of the Red Cavalry at war, their energy, fidelity, their violent natures. He wrote about a life of physical movement almost totally opposite his own sedentary youth and culture. He had the imagination to be just. It took all his strength, all his longing.

Babel would probably be called a minimalist today, but there's hardly a maximalist or mediumist who can tell a story, engage and shape a character with so much of the light and darkness of history, with grief *and* humor. The fact is, there's a larger, more varied population in Babel's four, five hundred pages of stories than in any three novels of most writers. A bald statement, to be proven another time.

❋

Red Cavalry is about men and what they expect of one another in the way of honor, physical courage, love of horses, abuse of women, and Jews. It's about a young man, a Russian too, but to them a foreigner, who is falling in love with their bravery and suffering. At the same time he is trying to give us the facts of the case. When women appear it's because of what men need to do *to* them as the men demand food and sex. The women are usually pregnant, which makes very little difference in the men's demands. The young man Babel doesn't shirk *his* honorable duty, which is to tell the story whole, as beautifully, that is as truthfully, as he can.

In the Odessa stories and others, some of which were written later, the women are able to . . . well, fly. Lyubka (called the Cossac, a Jewish woman) is wild and irascible, "a monstrous mother," and is in many ways more interesting than Benya Krik (the King). And this literary and historical and unbrutalized entrance of women allows for all kinds of humor and imagery ("meanwhile misfortune lurked under the window like a pauper at daybreak"). Which must have been a relief, because Babel liked to laugh.

"The Jewess" is a profound figure, forced with strong familial love out of her place and time by her son — into his. This story, had Babel had the time the times did not allow, might have become a novel.

Claudia in "Oil" is the head of the Oil Syndicate. She's a modern woman. We know her, her closeness to women friends, her great sense of humor, her political interest and brains. Was she a woman like Antonina Pirozhkova, an engineer who had a great deal to do with the building of the Moscow subway as well as assorted tunnels and bridges? In any case, it's good to have met these women. They must still be there, old and tough — I would like to meet them again.

But some stories, I must admit, you simply can't read more than once every couple of years, because in reading them, sorrow grips you so. An example would be the first story of *Red Cavalry*, "Crossing Over to Poland." Perhaps I feel this because it is so close to my parents' story of their own town's drowning in the 1905 manufactured waves of pogroms. The murder of my 17-year-old uncle Russya in that pogrom; the picture given to me many times of my grandmother, alone, bringing the wagon to his place of slaughter to lift his body, take him home. Within a few months she sent my young father and mother away with their Russian language to become Americans. There are only a few others, also wonderful, where the air of his normal hopefulness cannot raise the story out of heartsick sadness.

I see I have been a bit solemn, even in describing "Awakening," a story made famous by its humor — the large size of the violin cases, the small boys carrying them, the international hopes of the fathers, the narrow streets of the ghettos. Why is it that with the best intentions in the world, disparate size is comical except to the people involved, the unrequited lover of the disinterested and beautiful woman is a joke, at least until someone says, what's so funny about that? Heifetz and Zimbalist and Gabrilowitsch *did* come from Odessa. That's where they studied the violin. My son is also smart, maybe even gifted. Why do you laugh?

❋

THERE IS A KIND OF SUBGENRE (in which I have been implicated) called short shorts, which probably couldn't have happened without Babel's work. But what is missed much of the time is the density of that work. They are not pieces of life. They are each one *all* of life. Each one, even the shortest, is the story of a story.

Among other intentions I think Babel hoped to tell two kinds of stories — the first about lives absolutely unlike his own, in order to understand, or at least know and maybe even become like the "others."

But a second need was to say — look — that life is like mine. I am after all like him and he like me. What a relief! This happened from time to time. Here are two examples: In "The Story of the Horse," Klebnikov, the commander of the first squadron, has been deprived of his white stallion by Savitsky the Divisional Commander. He writes a letter of resignation from the Communist Party, beginning: "The Communist Party was founded, as I understand it, for joy and sound justice without limit, and it ought to consider small fry also. Now I will come to the question of the white stallion . . ." And Babel ends, ". . . he was a quiet fellow whose character was rather like mine. He was the only man in the squadron to possess a samovar . . . We used to drink scalding tea together. We were shaken by the same passions. Both of us looked on the world as a meadow in May — a meadow traversed by women and horses."

And at the end of "Sandy the Christ," after the son has made his bargain with his stepfather, Babel writes, "It was only recently that I got to know Sandy the Christ, and shifted my little trunk over to his cart. Since then we have often met the dawn and seen the sun set together. And whenever the capricious chance of war has brought us together, we have sat down of an evening on the bench outside a hut, or made tea in the woods in a sooty kettle, or slept side by side in the new-mown fields, the hungry horses tied to his foot or mine."

❈

IN THE MATTER OF HIS SMALL PRODUCTION (for some reason I feel this must be answered), apart from what I've said about the weight of its quality against the weight of the paper used by most writers, he had other journalistic and literary responsibilities.

He had to support his wife and child in France — they refused to return, wisely. He traveled with Pirozhkova on writing assignments to mining districts and to collectives — kolkhozes, where beet production was impressive, and to smaller fields where the agricultural leaders had turned to seed production for the whole region. (A few years later, he would learn that many of the working organizers of these successful projects had been arrested, maybe executed.) He also worked on many film scripts, once with Eisenstein, who was his good friend. He worked as a writer. That was his work.

We know that great boxes of his manuscripts were carted off by the NKVD. Among them, Pirozhkova is sure (and I am too), was his book to be called "New Stories." Did "they" fear these stories? He held them up for the usual scrutiny — one day or one year too long. We really don't know about his production.

We do know that we wish we had a lot more of his stories.

Babel and Pirozhkova could not have been blind to events. Early in 1918, Babel must have heard Gorky's warning, "Lenin, Trotsky, and their supporters have already been poisoned by the corruptive virus of power."

But they could not understand the confessions made again and again by people they admired. (Nor can anyone to this day quite take in the totality.) Pirozhkova, in her forthright way, asked why they didn't just stand up for what they believed if they disagreed with the directions taken. But Babel understood something. The Party — maybe they didn't want to see the Party go down. They had not yet included torture in their calculations, at least Babel said nothing about this to his wife. Still he must have understood that someone in charge did not love him. There were problems with publication of stories. He and Pasternak were not included among the Russian writers invited to the important cultural conference in Paris (the Congress for the Defense of Culture and Peace). Only after the French delegation furiously demanded their attendance were they allowed to appear. And again later, when Soviet prizes were given out to scientists and cultural figures, Babel and Pasternak were not honored.

After Gorky died in 1936, Babel said to Pirozhkova, "*Now* they won't let me live."

Still, almost to the end, until the moment of his arrest, he was considered influential. The wives and children of people arrested came to him asking that he intervene. He would try, but always returned grim-faced, not wanting to speak about it. He did not like to worry his wife. But he continued to offer care, and in more than one case shelter, to women whose husbands were in prison or had been executed. Many of his friends considered this unwise. When he was finally arrested, very few people called Antonina Pirozhkova or visited her again. Ilya Ehrenberg became the comforting exception.

Babel's grandmother had admonished: "You Must Know Everything." He did try. And eventually he knew a great deal. He knew war. He knew work. He knew love. He gave long classical reading lists to Pirozhkova. He didn't like literary talk. He didn't want to discuss his work.

Sad for her and sad for us. Maybe among his other thoughts, he hoped to protect her, a powerful and responsible working woman important in the construction of the new Soviet infrastructure. Was he also trying to save her from the destructive forces of disillusion? When Lion Feuchtwanger visited, she asked Babel what they'd talked about. "He spoke of his impressions of the USSR and of Stalin," he said. "He told me many bitter truths." Then Babel said no more.

For the most part I have tried to say something in these few pages about what I feel for Babel's work. It was the work of a man who, like the Gedali character from *Red Cavalry,* longed for the joy-giving revolution, thought he would wait as long as he could. He thought he could put his own joyful spirit out like an oar in history's river and deflect the revolution's iron boat by acting in a straightforward way for others. He thought laughter and jokes might work. In fact Pirozhkova learned that one of his arresters had been asked by the interrogator in charge, "Did he try to make a joke?"

Reading Pirozhkova's memoir, I feel I have come to know something of the man, to see Babel and his work in some common brilliant light of the hopeful revolution, unending love of *the* people as well as people, darkened at the edges by fate, the busy encroachment of evil. But Antonina Pirozhkova will tell you the whole story. Though she lived only seven years inside it, hardly an hour escaped her loving attention, and then her memory, and he is, as she was determined, restored to us — a great writer, a good man.

Grace Paley
August 12, 1996

INTRODUCTION

THE MEMOIR THAT FOLLOWS was written, in Russian, about the Soviet writer Isaac Babel by his second wife, Antonina Nikolaevna Pirozhkova. She writes of the years she knew him — from 1932 until his arrest in 1939 — and of the years afterward as she tried to learn of his fate. The memoir provides a kind a rare footage into the life of a writer about whom not much has been known and presents a man of wit, affection, charm, and mischief.

Isaac Emmanuilovich Babel was born in 1894 in Odessa. He grew up in a Jewish family of modest means and began writing early. He made a meteoric entrance into early Soviet literature with his Red Cavalry stories and then gained international fame as his stories were translated. They were in English by the late 1920s; Ernest Hemingway read them and reportedly told Ilya Ehrenburg that Babel "clots the curd better than I do." But Babel published less and less in the 1930s, and although at the first Congress of the Soviet Writers' Union in 1934 he joked about his becoming "a master of the genre of silence," it did not stop him from being arrested and killed. On the basis of not much more than a single volume of prose, he is a writer who has garnered praise as being the only prose writer of genius that the Soviet Union produced, a modern master of the short story and one of the greatest writers of the twentieth century.

Among readers who are familiar with his work, many are passionate in their admiration, but it must also be added that Babel is nowadays little known to the general reading public and that there has been no biography of him to date in any language. The most straightforward function of his widow's memoir is to help redress the absence of a biography.

Help redress, for Pirozhkova writes primarily of the seven years that she knew Babel and only on those events to which she was a witness. Critics and scholars have long speculated about these years, trying to account for Babel's much-diminished publication and subsequent arrest. Was he blocked as a writer, or so politically disaffected that he could not write or dared not publish; did he deliberately court danger? For scholars who have already read Pirozhkova's memoir in Russian when it first appeared in 1972 or in the 1989 uncensored edition, this English translation contains yet additional material that addresses these questions.

But for readers long familiar with Babel's work and with what has been available about him and his life — chiefly in the letters he wrote to his mother and sister in the West — there may be revelations ahead of a different order. In her portrayal of Babel, Pirozhkova catches his way of being full of surprises, usually in the service of merriment; and while this quality, like his legendary curiosity, will come as no surprise, it helps to bring Babel alive with a directness that should set the standard for any future biography. In terms of revelation, there's the matter of the author — a *second* wife? Babel's first marriage to Evgeniya Gronfein is well-known, she being the wife who left the USSR in 1925 for Paris, the wife he visited there a few times, one such visit resulting in the birth of his daughter Nathalie, who now lives in the United States and has long attended to the publication of her father's works in the West. Babel's visits abroad gave him opportunities to defect had he wanted to, which it seems he did not.

The memoir begins just at the point in Babel's life when he was about to go abroad and meet Nathalie for the first time, and though he pleaded with Evgeniya to return with him, she was adamant in her refusal. Sometime after his return to the Soviet Union, he was to start a new life with an attractive young woman in her twenties, a professional transport engineer who would work on the construction of the Moscow subway. This is Antonina Nikolaevna Pirozhkova, who became his second wife. She was fifteen years younger than Babel.

Of course, to speak of "marriage" requires both quotation marks and some clarification, since Babel never went through divorce proceedings with his first wife, nor did he take vows with Pirozhkova, but then it seems nobody in the USSR did at the time, weddings being regarded as bourgeois holdovers. She would not take his name, as she was using her own professionally, but when a daughter Lida was born to them in early 1937, she was given his name. Lida Babel, a professional architect, moved to the United States with her mother in 1996 to live in Maryland with Lida's married son, Andrei Malaev Babel, a director, actor, and drama teacher.

Surely, one reason that the existence of a second wife and family was little known in the West was that Babel never mentioned them in his frequent letters to his mother and sister. He was very fond of his mother; in fact, when he was arrested he expressed two regrets, which Pirozhkova, who was with him, sets down here: the first that he "wasn't allowed to finish," the second that his mother would stop receiving his letters. In the years before his arrest, he probably wished to spare his mother unhappy feelings over the failure of his marriage to Evgeniya, especially since his mother seemed to feel an enduring awe over this union connecting the Babel family with the eminent Gronfeins. So there was no mention of Antonina Nikolaevna or Lida in letters that would someday be read by Babel's admirers around the world. Needless to say, there had also been no mention years earlier of a love affair that Babel had with the actress Tamara Kashirina shortly before his wife departed for Paris — one that resulted in the birth of a boy, Misha, born on Babel's birthday, July 13, 1926. He was "lost" to Babel when his mistress married the writer Vsevolod Ivanov, who adopted the boy. Misha Ivanov is still alive in Moscow today, and appears in the memoir.

That Babel did not write of her in family letters did not bother Antonina Nikolaevna at all, she told me in a series of interviews in 1990. It was what he wanted; she understood why and she agreed, for clearly she adored him. Adoration drives what she has written, adoration mixed with veneration and perhaps a touch of fear. She never disobeyed his rule that she not look at his rough drafts, and she always addressed him with the formal "vy" (you), which he used with her too, as though it were a game.

Besides, his family was abroad, far away and part of the past, while her own young career in the early 1930s likely felt, for a long stretch of time, like an unbroken series of triumphant breakthroughs. She was born in 1909 in Siberia, of parents who were members of the intelligentsia and who had moved "out

East" from Belarus. (Her mother grew up in the town of Lyubavitch, where she had so many Jewish girlfriends that she knew enough Yiddish to join in teasing the boys about their sidecurls.) Pirozhkova did well at school not only in literature, "as expected," but in mathematics, at which she was exceptionally gifted, and in the decade following the Russian Revolution she attended university and took a degree in construction engineering. It was still an unusual thing to do for any woman anywhere, and as it happened the timing could not have been better for the study of engineering, for the young country was in such need of specialists that an engineering student might be asked to go build a bridge somewhere in order to complete a course requirement. Within a few months of graduation she was employed at the Kuznetsk Metallurgical plant, and one could even argue that thanks to the times — the early 1930s under Stalin, with the tentative beginnings of purge trials — her education was about to continue. For at the Kuznetsk plant she was to meet a group of engineer-intellectuals from Moscow or Leningrad, many of whom had recently returned from Siberia where they had been sent to work off some political misstep. These men included her in their frequent gatherings where they recited poetry and discussed literature, and they introduced her to the works of contemporary writers, including the much-acclaimed Isaac Babel. A year and a half later, on a trip to Moscow, she was to meet Babel in person, at a luncheon given by an official who had taken notice of her at Kuznetsk Metallurgical.

Obviously, it was not hard to notice her. She was the solitary female construction-engineer, very good at her job, and very attractive. In one photograph of her and Babel together she has a wry, intelligent smile and looks very much like Isadora Duncan, who had been in Moscow and whom Babel had known in her incarnation as Mrs. Sergei Esenin. In the photo Babel looks paunchy, happy, and a little goggle-eyed; he did not photograph well, but by numerous accounts he was much pursued by women. He might have been drawn to her, of course, just by her beauty, but from her accounts of their first meetings there are signs that other qualities may have "made" the match. Babel had an appetite for merriment, and she too had a taste for hilarity, seen early on when she burst into laughter at his offer, made very seriously, of a ruble for every letter received that she would let him read. From his first invitation to lunch, promising *varenniki* with cherries, she joins him in enjoying what is delicious. Sometimes she would remember the visit of a foreign writer, like André Gide, by what they served for supper and then by what Babel said about their guest. Being a professional, she was busy and gave him the solitude necessary for writing, and being a professional engineer, she didn't bother him with literary talk, which he hated. In fact, she protected him from it on occasion. She was of the new generation at work on the "unprecedented" country with which he had cast his lot, and she may have represented to him his tenure in the Soviet present and his place in its future.

As for her, trained professional but also child of the intelligentsia, she clearly knew the kind of company now opening to her. In her profession she had flown straight to the top by being chosen to work on the project of the day, building the Moscow subway, and the work likely gave her steady footing in Babel's world, as well as income and a sense of her own competence, for she was meeting many of the foremost artists of the time, Russian and foreign. Figures like Eisenstein, Pasternak, Malraux, H. G. Wells — even Stalin — are portrayed or glimpsed at functions attended, which is to say, her memoir also gives us a picture of life among Soviet artists and intellectuals in the 1930s.

One is tempted to speculate if it was the combination of the skills developed in both worlds she inhabited that made the most unusual aspects of Pirozhkova's memoir possible. A mathematics-primed memory was essential. She knew a good line when she heard one. She had colleagues at work to whom she would quote what Babel had said the day before, and years later, though she had kept no diary, she was able to write down things he said in the idiosyncratic and unmistakable way he said them. Her memoir brings us more Babel.

Babel's previously unspoken political opinions will not be found here. He did not confide in her, perhaps to keep her safe, perhaps because he confided in no one. The one exception was the expression of his bewilderment that people they knew were confessing in prison to incredible and unlikely acts — but then, Pirozhkova writes, she and Babel were still unable to believe that torture was being used in Soviet prisons.

But there is much more about Babel than we have previously had. Sometimes it emerges obliquely, as when she describes a reading list Babel gave her of those books he considered essential. His list, from Greek and Roman classics to Western European literature, besides reading like a modern-day "great books" syllabus, throws unexpected light on Babel's intellectual scope, the nonparochial range of mind that would have set him apart from so many of his peers. To think of him, tutored in Suetonius, observing the operation of great and deadly power at close range, offers us a new perspective on his life and work.

In terms of how he worked as an artist, what the memoir brings us will counter older portraits that have Babel writing huge numbers of drafts of each story. Pirozhkova describes him in states of trance-like absorption, pacing his room, winding and unwinding string on his fingers, stopping to jot down something. And she does address directly the old questions of whether Babel's productivity in the 1930s was so diminished. By her account, it was not. He wrote a great deal, did scenarios for films to get by financially, and was writing a piece of fiction around a Benia Krik-like character, to be called Kolya Topuz, who struggles to adjust to collectivization. When Babel was arrested in May of 1939 he was finishing a new collection of stories due out in the fall, but in the course of his arrest all papers and manuscripts were seized.

Yet, and almost despite everything just mentioned involving Babel, literary people, or his creative work, one should qualify that this is not a literary memoir. Pirozhkova writes in a straightforward manner as an eyewitness account of what she experienced at the side of a man whom she held to be great in human stature, and who was also a great writer. She makes no attempt, even in hindsight, to embrace his career as a writer; there is no mention of works published in "her" time, such as the stories "Guy de Maupassant" or "Di Grasso," which stand large in the canon of his work. There is no mention of the fate or significance of the film Babel and Eisenstein worked on together, *Bezhin Meadow* (which is about collectivization and has nothing to do with the Turgenev story of the same name). Pirozhkova writes of the trip south to see the film being shot, Babel's struggles to keep Eisenstein down to earth, his admiration for the rushes — but no mention that Eisenstein had requested that Babel rewrite the first scenario entirely so that he had to reshoot almost everything, or that the film was finally destroyed or repressed and that Eisenstein was later to call this the greatest tragedy of his creative life.

With Babel's arrest, of which she gives a riveting account, almost everything in Pirozhkova's life was to change. She continued to work, which gave her income and might well have saved her from arrest. At home, a boorish NKVD investigator and his wife were settled in Babel's vacated room, and while she was treated with respect at work, at home she was addressed only as an "enemy of the people," and this was to last seventeen years. Some friends of Babel's whom she had earlier disliked for not paying attention to her, such as Ilya Ehrenburg, now became close friends. They offered her what help they could, while she was grateful that they continued to revere Babel as she did.

Though she was encouraged to believe that Babel was still alive in prison camps, from the time of the arrest she put on the Soviet cloak of widowhood, and her memoir includes the dark and solitary years as she raised their child while she tried to send help, locate him, learn his fate, then struggle to clear his name ("rehabilitation"), then press to have his works republished, transcribe a rescued copy of his 1920 war diary, and eventually publish this memoir. She did all this, wedding vows or no, as his second wife, and when she writes about the years — the decades — after his arrest, she is writing as much about Babel's literary fate as about how she managed her own life.

The appearance of this memoir has its own three-part history, which Pirozhkova discusses, but which deserves some additional commentary. When the volume of reminiscences was being put together, with contributions from eminent contemporaries of Babel's, Pirozhkova was involved with editing the essays and she never intended to write one herself. She explained to me in 1990 that when all the submissions were received, she suddenly felt Babel was not there. She then decided to write, and her long memoir was well received by the scholars in charge; it was also censored by the publishing authorities. In 1989, the volume was reissued with the censored parts restored, some new additions, and Pirozhkova at the helm soliciting new work. When foreign publishers then asked to publish her memoir alone in translation, she added nearly another thirty typescript pages. Everything appears here.

Here I can add a brief personal note as an eyewitness to the memoir's progress to full appearance. In 1975, when I was a graduate student studying in Moscow, I visited Antonina Nikoleavna, whom I had met several years earlier at her home and expressed admiration for her memoir, which I had read in New York in 1972. She asked if I would like to read the uncensored version and brought out a thick typescript. It was not difficult; you had to leaf through until you came to a paragraph or half-page or page next to which a line and an "x" were neatly drawn in blue pencil. The penciled paragraphs or sections amounted to about eleven pages, memorable both for their contents as well as for the close-up view they gave of Soviet censorship at work. Encounters with foreign acquaintances, especially Chinese, were omitted. Then there was a category of episodes obviously judged improper or risqué, such as her discovery of Eisenstein's erotic photographs turned against the wall when Babel brought her on a visit, or even Babel's words of gratitude to her when she rescued him from a squad of pestering journalists: "Go wash your feet, I'll drink the bathwater." Anything politically sensitive was out, which is to say the entire account of Babel's arrest was deleted.

All was restored and expanded when the volume of reminiscences was reissued in 1989, but here history intervened with further disclosures, for the same liberalization that had allowed Pirozhkova to speak openly of Babel's arrest now opened access to the archives of the secret police. In December of 1988 a commission was created by the literary community for "the Artistic

Legacy of Suppressed Writers," and its deputy chairman, Vitali Shentalinski, found in the secret police archives, among many other files, "Case #419, Babel, I. E." He wrote up and published its contents in the periodical *Ogonyok* (Number 39) in 1989, and later in book form. The first publication came within months of the new edition of Pirozhkova's memoir, in which her belief that Babel had been alive as late as the summer of 1952 in a labor camp in the Kolyma region was left unamended.

Summarized, the facts of Case #419 are awful enough: arrested May 15, 1939, Babel was held in Moscow prisons (first the Lubyanka, then Butyrka) for eight months, interrogated many times, a case against him built as a spy and part of an antigovernment Trotskyite conspiracy; then in January 1940, in a twenty-minute trial he was sentenced to death, and the sentence was carried out the next day, January 27th. This date unseats the question mark given in place of a definite year of death in the parentheses after his name in every book, anthology, and encyclopedia entry until now.

But the details of what Babel had to endure make the account even worse. At the initial interrogation in late May of 1939, Babel began by adamantly denying any wrongdoing, but then after three days he suddenly "confessed" to what his interrogator was suggesting and named many people as co-conspirators. In all likelihood he was tortured, almost certainly beaten. A photograph of Babel included in Case #419, and published in *Ogonyok* with the caption "the last photograph of Isaac Babel," shows him without glasses, his face looking bruised. Whether his glasses were taken from him or smashed, without them he would have been virtually blind. At subsequent interrogations he readily agreed to whatever was put forward as plots he took part in. After a month there was enough evidence to bring him to trial, but an extension was requested by the interrogator, then this interrogator was replaced, and more months went by. In August, Babel wrote a letter to Lavrenti Beria, the new head of the secret police, requesting that he be allowed to put his seized manuscripts in order, representing as they did "eight years of creative work." There was no reply. In October, summoned for interrogation, Babel denied all of his previous testimony. A statement was recorded: "I ask the inquiry to take into account that, though in prison, I committed a crime. I slandered several people."

Its work wrecked, the interrogators quickly rebuilt the case using the "testimony" of others who had been arrested, and again there was a lapse of time. (War was just breaking out in Europe at this time, and it is possible that the Kremlin, knowing of Hitler's plans in advance, was waiting for the distraction of war to prevent any protest in Europe over the arrests of figures like Babel. Vsevolod Meyerhold, the great theater director, was arrested at about the same time.) Babel now began writing letters — on scraps of paper, in an unsteady hand — to the chief prosecutor of the USSR, first asking "to be heard" (on November 5th) for the chance to make a statement of "unusual significance" to his case. Receiving no reply, he wrote again (on November 21st), trying to make sure that no one be injured with suspicion because of his testimony, albeit retracted. He wrote in a language of careful and correct officalese, professing concern with the investigation above all, while at the same time expressing great personal anguish. "The thought that my words not only serve to hinder this investigation but might bring my country direct harm causes me unspeakable suffering. My primary obligation as I see it is to remove this terrible stain from my conscience." There was no response and he wrote again, elaborating further. "The thought that my testimonies not only do not serve the matter of clarifying the truth but are leading

the investigation to mistaken conjectures torments me uncease-
lessly . . . I ascribed anti-Soviet acts and tendencies to the writer
I. Ehrenburg (and others) . . . All this is untrue and has no basis
whatsoever. I knew these people to be honest and staunch Soviet
citizens. The slander was called forth by my faintheartedness
during the interrogation."

Up to the day before his trial he wrote letters to officials of
the tribunal, asking for witnesses at this trial, but especially asking to clear from any slander "entirely guiltless people." Given
the chance to speak at this trial, he spoke less obliquely about his
"faintheartedness during interrogation." "I am not guilty," he
said. "I was no spy. I never tolerated a single act against the
Soviet Union. On certain occasions while giving testimony I cast
aspersions on myself. I slandered myself and others under
duress." These were his last words recorded at the trial, and the
last words we have of him.

Readers may find an uncanny fit between Pirozhkova's
memoir and the secret police file, the first going with Babel to
the door of the Lubyanka, the second following him inside. But
the two fit together in another way, for when read together the
memoir illuminates some moments of Babel's ordeal, giving
them unexpected and tragic dimensions. The description of
Babel denying any wrongdoing at the start of his interrogation,
as of course he would have, recalls the passage in the memoir
when he recounts a conversation with Yagoda, then head of the
secret police. In order to fill an awkward silence Babel asks,
"How should someone act if he falls into your men's paws?"
"Deny everything," Yagoda advised. "If one denies everything,
we are powerless." Those words go with Babel into prison, but
the advice failed him.

The account of Babel confessing "under duress," under
some form of torture, recalls the passage in the memoir that

describes how puzzled he was to hear of the wild confessions of people he knew to be innocent. If before his arrest he did not believe torture could be used in Soviet prisons, then a part of his ordeal had to be one of grim understanding, understanding why others had acted as they did and how his own assumptions had been betrayed. If in his confession Babel named as co-conspirators many of the people who figure in the memoir, artists like Eisenstein, Ehrenburg, and the actor Mikhoels, then Pirozhkova's portrayal of the friendships, so rich in affection and admiration, made what was to transpire — Babel's retraction and his repeated attempts to clear his friends from suspicion — not only understandable but desperately urgent.

Pirozhkova's speculations and conclusions about the circumstances of Babel's end were revised in this, the third version of her memoir. We have not only her revision but her response to finally learning, after fifty years of inquiry, how her husband died. It is a credit to her memoir, and a measure of the force with which she brings Babel so clearly to life, that her anguish is so palpable.

Her memoir is about how Babel lived his last years and after that how she lived without him. As for the rest of the story that comes from the secret police files, the workings of the machinery of terror have been documented many times before but have rarely been more wrenching, because the victim has been summoned to full liveliness so well that his presence is both irrefutable and unbearable to lose.

Anne Frydman
July 25, 1996

I WISH TO RESTORE TO PUBLIC MEMORY certain features of a man endowed with great goodness of spirit, a passionate interest in people, and a miraculous gift for depicting them, since I had the good fortune to live by Isaac Babel's side for a few years. These reminiscences are a simple record of facts as yet little known in the literature on Babel — his thoughts, words, actions and his encounters with people from various walks of life — to which I was witness.

I met him in the summer of 1932, about a year after first reading his stories. We were introduced at the Moscow home of Ivan Pavlovich Ivanchenko, the President of Vostokostal (Eastern Steel Works). Ivan Pavlovich, a great admirer of Babel's work, had invited both of us for lunch on the same day. Ivan Pavlovich knew me from the Kuznetsk Construction Project, where I had worked after graduating from the Siberian Institute for

Transport Engineers. Whenever he came to Moscow, he and his sister stayed at the Donbass Miners' House on 26 Petrovka Street.

Babel arrived a little late for lunch and explained that he had come straight from the Kremlin where he had just received permission to visit his family in France. Ivanchenko introduced me to Babel by saying, "Here's a construction engineer who goes by the name of Princess Turandot."

That was what Ivanchenko always called me since the time he had come to Kuznetsk Construction and read a bulletin board article critical of me entitled "Princess Turandot from the Construction Department."

Babel looked at me with a smile and some surprise, and all through lunch he kept coaxing me to drink vodka with him. "If a woman's an engineer, and a construction engineer no less, then she has to be able to drink vodka." Unwilling to damage the reputation of my fellow construction-engineers, I had no choice but to drink the vodka down — without making a face.

Over lunch Babel told us how difficult it had been for him to get permission to go abroad and how long the process had dragged on. Going was an absolute necessity for him since his family lived abroad with no means of support, and it was very difficult to help them from Moscow.

"I'm going there to meet a little three-year-old French miss," he said. "I'd like to bring her back to Russia, as I fear they might turn her into a monkey there." He was speaking of his daughter Natasha, whom he had not yet seen.

A few days later, when Ivan Pavlovich left for Magnitogorsk, Babel invited Ivanchenko's sister and me to his home for lunch, promising us there would be cheese dumplings (*vareniki*), with cherries.

The name of the lane that Babel lived on was one I found

striking — Great Nikolo-Vorobinsky (Great Lane of Nikola and the Sparrows). When I asked how it had gotten such a strange name, Babel offered the following explanation.

"It comes from the church, 'Nikolai-on-the-Sparrows' — the one almost across from the house. The church was apparently built with the help of sparrows, that is to say, in order to raise money for its construction, sparrows were caught, cooked, and sold."

I found this surprising but decided it could be so. There was, after all, Moscow's Church of the Trinity, which by legend had been built with drops of vodka, or rather with the money gotten from drops of vodka left in glasses, with which a tavern-owner had had the church built. Later I was to learn that both the lane and the church across from Babel's house were not named for sparrows, *vorob'i*, but for *voroby*, spindles used in olden times.

Babel's apartment itself was as unusual as the lane's name. It had two floors, with a foyer, dining room, study, and kitchen on the first floor, and bedrooms on the second. Babel explained that he shared the apartment with an Austrian engineer named Bruno Aloizovich Shtainer, and he told us the history of their acquaintance and shared living quarters. Shtainer was the chief representative of an Austrian firm named Elin that sold electrical equipment to the Soviet Union. Several officials represented the firm and together they had occupied the entire apartment. Then our country decided that it no longer needed the Austrian equipment, and it was arranged for only one representative — Shtainer — to remain in Moscow as a consultant to Soviet engineers. Left by himself and worried that the six-room apartment would be taken away, Shtainer began looking for a companion who could defend it. He was good friends with the writer Lidiya Seifulina, and asked her to find him someone from among the writers she knew. Seifulina recommended Babel, who at the time had no apartment and was crammed in at his friend's house.

"And that was how I came to be here on Nikolo-Vorobinsky," Babel said. "We each took two rooms upstairs, and we share the dining room and study downstairs. Shtainer and I have a 'gentleman's agreement': we divide all expenses for food and upkeep, and we allow absolutely no women on the premises. Shtainer has just left Moscow for Vienna where he'll be staying for a long time."

I was to visit Nikolo-Vorobinsky a few more times before Babel himself left to go abroad. Once he said to me, "Come for lunch tomorrow and I'll introduce you to a very witty man."

The next day, when I arrived at Babel's apartment, the guest, who turned out to be Nikolai Robertovich Erdman,* was already there. My arrival interrupted the conversation, but he and Babel quickly resumed it. I listened in with interest and learned that they were talking about Erdman's play that had been refused production.

The play in question was Erdman's *The Suicide*.† Babel told me briefly what it was about and then added, "It's a play with a rather gloomy title, but it is literally bursting with jokes about contemporary life, and people are calling it the new *Woe from Wit*."††

After lunch, Babel kept insisting that I talk about my work at Kuznetsk Construction in 1931. I told a story about a request that had come to my construction division from the office of a coal mine. They needed a consultant who was a specialist in founda-

---

* Nikolai Robertovich Erdman (1902–1970), Russian-Soviet writer.
† The play was to be staged by the Meyerhold Theatre in Moscow in October, 1932 but was banned by the government following the dress rehearsal.
†† Aleksandr Griboedov's classic Russian comedy of 1833.

tions and substructures. The head of our division assigned me to go after warning me that the engineers there were all exiles who had been convicted in the Shakhty trial of 1928*. The only way to get there was by horse-drawn sled, a drive of about thirty kilometers. I was met by respectable-looking men with beards wearing identical peaked caps and sheepskin jackets. The problem turned out to a very trivial one: they needed to build a one-story structure for a new office, but the soil base was loess, which has the particular feature of soaking up water. At the Kuznetsk Metallurgical Factory all the blast furnaces and shops had been built on the very same loess, and I was amused to learn this was the reason these eminent engineers had called in a consultant to advise them on such an insignificant matter. And the consultant was barely twenty-two-years old.

After I had described the problem and produced a blueprint for a building plan, they invited me to join them for a luncheon at the home of a man who apparently ran the coal mine. The apartment was furnished with antiques, it had paintings hung on the log-cabin walls, a carpet on the floor and there was even a piano. The table was magnificently set. The engineers' wives, ladies in old-fashioned dresses and diamond earrings, appeared beside the proper men in their mining-engineering uniforms. It was all incredible to find in such a backwater.

When I had finished the story, Babel said, "You see, Nikolai Robertovich, of course those engineers knew perfectly well how to do everything, but they deliberately refused to take on responsibility of any kind. If they were not going to be trusted, then let it be the Bolsheviks who answer for decisions. That was

---

* Engineers working at Shakhty and other sites in the Donets Basin, a coal mining region, were accused of counterrevolutionary economic sabotage. The trials took place in Moscow.

why they staged the whole comedy...Well, tell us some more now."

So I told them about something that had happened at Kuznetsk Construction in the winter of 1931 when the brick-working division had had to put up two blast-furnace smokestacks at the same time. Each smokestack was being built by a separate brick-laying brigade, and the two brigades competed fiercely with each other. Everyone — not just we engineers, but every worker in every division, and even all the housewives watching from their windows — all came out to watch the competition. Everyone became involved, argued about which brigade would finish first, made bets. No one was indifferent, everyone was caught up in the excitement. Both brigades were identical in strength, so first the bricks would get higher on one smokestack, then on the other, and all this was happening high up where everyone could see.

After my story, Babel commented: "Ah, to write it down the way she tells it! These days they write about competitions — and it's solid boredom."

Once Babel asked if I would let him come visit me at my place. I made a pot of tea for him, not very strong as I recall (later I was to learn that he liked his tea as strong as possible), but he drank it without comment. And then he suddenly said, "Would you let me see what you have in your purse?"

Extremely surprised, I agreed.

"Thank you. You see, I'm terribly interested in what ladies carry in their purses."

Very carefully he set out the contents of my purse on the table, examined each thing and then put it back, except for a letter which I had just received that day from an engineering institute classmate. This he set aside. He looked at me with a serious expression and said, "Would you perhaps let me read this letter too, unless, of course, it is dear to you for some special reason?"

"Go ahead, read it," I said.

He read it closely and then asked: "Could I make an arrangement with you? I'll give you a ruble for every letter you receive and let me read." All this in complete seriousness. Here I burst out laughing and agreed, so Babel pulled out a ruble and put it on the table.

※

BABEL TOLD ME THAT most of the time he did not live in Moscow, where it was hard to find the solitude necessary for work, but instead he stayed in the village of Molodenovo, near Gorky's house in Gorki. He invited me to go out there the next time I had a day off from work.

He called for me early in the morning and we went down to Belorussian Station to catch a train. We got off at Zhavoronok where a horse and carriage were waiting for us, something Babel had obviously arranged in advance. The road took us first through a cluster of summer cottages, then through fields, then through a grove of oak trees. Babel was in very good spirits, and for some reason told me a story about a husband bringing his wife home from their wedding. Along the way, when the husband's horse had refused to obey him on the count of "one," and again on the count of "two," after the count of "three" he had hacked the animal to death. This made such an impression on his wife that from then on her husband had only to say "one" for her to carry out his command at once, remembering what followed "three."

The house that Babel lived in was on the very outskirts of town and stood at the edge of a ravine. A little stream flowed at the bottom, emptying eventually into the Moscow River. Inside the vestibule of the house two doors led off to separate wings.

The first, occupied by the landlord, Ivan Karpovich, and his family, was made up of a kitchen, living room, and a bedroom facing the street. The second, in which Babel lived, consisted of just one big room whose windows faced the kitchen garden. It was furnished very modestly, with a simple table, two or three stools, and two narrow beds in the corners.

Babel was determined to show me all the sights of Molodenovo, so we started off right away on foot to see the stud farm. There we were shown the newly foaled colts, even one who had been born just the night before and was named "Vera, come back!" for the wife of one of the trainers who had left him for another man.

We looked all around the stud farm, where everyone knew Babel and wanted to tell him everything in complete detail, which I found surprising and for some reason amusing. Then we headed over to see the mares in foal, which were grazing separately on the banks of the Moscow River.

The conversation Babel had with a trainer there was highly specialized and full of expressions that I was to understand only much later — "high runner," "having a fine exterior," "leading by a nose." It seemed to me that Babel had forgotten all about me. Finally, he came over and started talking about the mares. The first filly was, in his words, a complete hysteric; the second was a prostitute; the third one managed to produce first-rate offspring no matter how poor the sire, i.e., she improved the breed, while the fourth, as a general rule, made it worse.

Both on the way to the stud farm and on the way back we walked past the gate of a white house with columns where Maksim Gorky lived. Past the house, we turned off the road and went down to the river, and after a swim we headed back to

Molodenovo through a magnificent birch grove. Then Babel took me to meet an old beekeeper, a very tall man with a large beard who was a confirmed Tolstoyan and a vegetarian. He gave us tea to drink and honey in honeycombs.

We again returned to the railway station by horse and carriage. On the way, Babel said to me: "Here you are, an educated young lady who has just spent the day with a rather well-known writer, and you haven't asked him even one literary question." Without letting me answer, he said: "You were perfectly right to do so."

Later I came to fully understand how much Babel disliked talking about literature, which he would do almost anything to avoid.

Babel was very familiar with the operations of the Molodenovo *kolkhoz*, or collective farm, as he had even helped run it for awhile before we met. He had not done this for money, of course, but just to learn about life on a *kolkhoz*. Everyone there called him Manuilych.*

Not long before he went off to France, Babel persuaded me to move to Nikolo-Vorobinsky during his stay abroad. He was afraid that during the interim someone might be moved into the empty apartment. Shtainer was still abroad at the time. Babel was hopeful that, if it proved necessary, I would be able to find people who could defend the apartment against being filled with strangers. I moved into one of Babel's rooms upstairs and lived there for five or six months with a fine young woman named Ellie, Schteiner's maid.

Babel remained in France for so long that it began to be rumored in Moscow that he was never returning. When I wrote to him about this he wrote back saying, "What can people, who do

---

* This affectionate nickname was derived from Babel's patronymic name, Emmauilovich.

not know anything, possibly say to you, who knows everything?" Babel wrote from France often, almost daily. I accumulated many letters from him during his 11-month absence. When Babel was arrested in 1939 all of these letters were confiscated and never returned to me.

Once during the spring of 1933 I visited Molodenovo with Efim Aleksandrovich Draitser and when I described this visit to Babel, he wrote: "The knife of jealousy was turned in my heart when you wrote of your visit. In my longing for home, Molodenovo is the place that appears before my eyes."

Babel also wrote that he had been commissioned to write a scenario for a film about the double agent Azef, and that he had agreed so that he could earn some money to leave behind for his family. He mentioned this several times in his letters, but some years later when I tried to find out from Babel's sister and his daughter Natasha whether he had written the screenplay and, if so, what had become of it, they could tell me nothing about it. Only in 1966 when Olga Eliseevna Kolbasina, the widow of V.M. Chernov, the Socialist revolutionary, came to Moscow from Paris did I learn that she and Babel had written the scenario together. This was because Azev used to visit the Chernovs regularly, and so she knew him well. As I recall, she said that two scenes had been completed. Babel used to dictate them to her. She promised to find these scenes among her papers, but shortly afterward she died in Moscow. She had left all her papers in Paris with her daughter, Natalia Viktorovna Rez, whom I also asked to look for the scenes. If memory serves me, and, indeed, I may be mistaken, the work on the screenplay ended when some other party offered the movie studio a completed script on the same theme.

In 1933 Babel returned from abroad. He came alone — without his family. At that time I arranged to leave my current

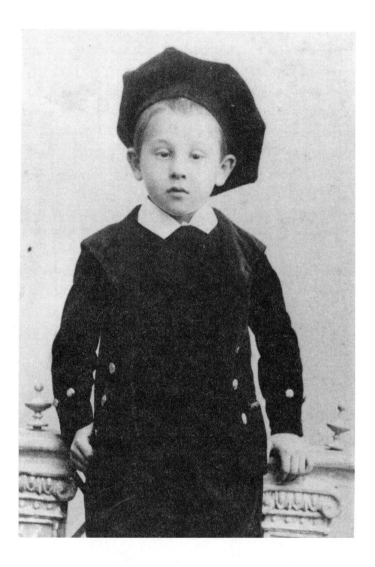

Babel, 1899.

job so that, after a vacation, I could start working on something more interesting. I had planned to spend my vacation in Sochi at a resort. When Babel learned this, he advised me to spend my time traveling along the Caucasus sea coast. He himself wanted to show me the area, including Kabardino – Balkariya and the so-called "Mineral Group" — Kislovodsk, Pyatigorsk, and Zheleznovodsk. We agreed that Babel would come to get me in Sochi toward the end of my stay.

I met him at the Sochi railway station and we headed off to the Riviera to spend a few days in a hotel. Once we had settled in, we started to plan our itinerary. We decided to start with a visit to Gagry where they were shooting the film *Merry Fellows*. Its scenario was by Erdman and Mass, and the actor Utyosov* had a lead role. After Gagry we planned to go off to Sukhumi and then to Kabardino-Balkarya. I told Babel that I had a first-class ticket from Sochi to Moscow that would go to waste.

"That's all right," he replied. "We'll exchange it for two tickets to Armavir."

The next day we were eating lunch at a table with two elderly women, one of whom was complaining to her companion that she was having no luck getting a ticket to Moscow. Suddenly, Babel spoke up.

"We've got a ticket to Moscow we don't need."

Without saying a word, I took the ticket out of my purse and handed it to this total stranger.

"How much do I owe you?" she asked.

"Nothing, it's free — please take it, it's of no use to us whatsoever," Babel replied.

---

* Leonid Osipovich Utyosov (1895–1982), Odessa-born "vaudeville" actor.

I could sense that he was dreadfully upset. After all, he did not really know me very well, so he couldn't know how I would react. Hadn't we just yesterday decided to exchange this ticket for two tickets to Armavir? Obviously disturbed, he kept glancing up at me while I kept chattering away as though the whole matter was of no importance.

Babel's kindness bordered on the catastrophic. I became convinced of this later on — the ticket incident being just the first example. Whenever such circumstances arose, he could not control himself. He would give away his watch, his shirts, his ties, saying: "If I want possessions, it's only so that I can give them away." But then he could also give my things away. For example, when he returned from France, he brought me a camera. A few months later, a photographer he knew was going north on a field trip, and when the man told Babel that he did not possess a camera, Babel immediately gave him mine. I never saw it again.

Whenever Babel would give my things away, he would inevitably feel upset and guilty, but I knew that he could not restrain himself. While I never let him know that I regretted losing my possessions, the truth was, of course, that I did.

It was on a warm sunny day that we left for Gagry in a convertible with its top down. It was still morning when we noticed that a covered black car with a small barred window on the side passed us going the other way. We noticed it, but that was all. However, when we reached Gagry we found that the whole film troop was upset: Erdman had just been arrested. Why? Possibly, because of a fable he had written.

While we were still in Sochi Babel told me that he was looking forward to the pleasure of two meetings in particular — one with Erdman, another with Utesov. He found the news of Erdman's arrest both shocking and deeply upsetting.

There were no vacant rooms in the Gagripsh Hotel. However, Erdman's little room under the staircase had just come free, and it was given to me. Babel moved in with Utesov. In the room that had been Erdman's there was still an open book and a package of cigarettes lying on a night stand next to the bed.

Everyone was crushed. The actress, Mashenka Strelkova, wanted to cry, but her long artificial eyelashes got in the way. Writer Aleksandr Nikolaevich Tikhonov (Serebrov) walked about in a sombre mood. It was only years later that I learned from Erdman that he had actually been transported in an ordinary, uncovered bus and that he had seen us in our car. For our part, we had paid no attention to the oncoming bus.

Erdman also told me that when they had arrested him he was wearing luxurious white trousers and a white silk shirt, whereas his jail cell had no furniture. Having paced this empty cell for a long time, he finally decided to stretch out on the dirty floor. At a bus stop on the way to Sochi they had let him buy some grapes and that was all he had eaten until evening. On the other hand he fared much better on the train to Moscow. The NKVD officers rewarded him with black caviar, smoked salmon, ham, and even cognac.*

Meanwhile back at Gagry, the filming of *Merry Fellows* continued. Babel and I went to see them shoot Utesov and the actress Orlova, and to watch as the lovely actress Tiapkina flopped into the water over and over. Utesov boasted of an increasing number of female admirers, and I found this so irritating that I told him, "I don't know what they see in you, you're not good looking, and frankly, I don't think you're anything special."

---

* After his arrest, Erdman was sentenced to exile in Siberia and didn't return to Moscow until the late 1930s. After this "warning," he did not write another serious work.

Utesov immediately blew up and went to Babel to complain.

"She doesn't find me good looking — well, you'd better set her straight on that score, and just let her know who she's dealing with here!"

So I had to listen while Babel lectured me. "You shouldn't be so frank. Besides, he's artistic from head to toe. You've seen him act — why, he's even artistic from the rear."

I did not agree with Babel at all, so I left and spent the whole day wandering through the Zhoekvarskoe gorge, which impressed me with its wild beauty. The following day I talked Babel into going off on a mountain trek.

Gradually, without letting him know it, I took him off to the gorge. There was one spot where we had to walk a narrow path and, following the protrusion of the cliff above a precipice, the only way to advance was to edge sideways with our backs flush against the wall of the cliff. Suddenly, I became extremely fearful for Babel. I grabbed his hand and, without looking down, we made it past the dangerous spot.

Having caught his breath on the pathway down to the sea, Babel said: "Susanin — where have you brought me?" * It had already turned dark by the time we had descended the mountain. We were terribly hungry, so as soon as we found a local inn we went in and ordered spicy mutton soup that we ate with white, aromatic bread. It seemed impossible to imagine anything more delicious.

Babel loved to walk, but since he suffered from asthma he had to start off gradually, after which he could then cover a fair distance. Back then I didn't yet know this and had taken him off on a long mountain hike without giving him a chance to adjust

---

* A reference to M. I. Glinka's opera, *Ivan Susanin,* where Susanin tricks the Polish forces into following him off into the woods. Although Susanin is killed, the Poles also perish.

his breathing. He was having trouble breathing and felt terrible overall, although he tried to hide this from me.

❋

DURING OUR EVENINGS IN GAGRY we used to visit a Persian named Kurban. There, sitting under plane trees, we would drink strong hot tea served with medlar jam.

During this stay, Utesov was an inexhaustible fount of stories. I learned for the first time that he was not only a talented musician, but also a talented storyteller who had given public readings of Babel's "How It Was Done in Odessa" and "Salt." Once he gave Babel his photograph with the humorous inscription: "To the only man who overstands our life." *

At Gagry, Babel wanted to meet with Nestor Lakoba, the President of the Abkhazian Central Executive Committee. I accompanied him to the Central Committee dacha where Lakoba was vacationing. There, on a bench near the entrance, I waited for Babel.

The meeting with Lakoba lasted about an hour, after which the two emerged, talked a bit more, and then said good-bye. I was struck by Lakoba's wearing a dark suit on such a sunny day and the hearing-aid cord by his ear. On the way home Babel said that Nestor Lakoba was the most remarkable man in all Abkhaziya.

In 1984 I received a letter from Stanislav Lakoba, a relative of Nestor's, informing me that on the 26th of December, 1936, Beria,† while visiting Tbilisi, had had Lakoba poisoned. Beria's wife had helped by lacing Lakoba's wine with the poison.

---

* *"Ponimavshii za zhiza"* — a comically ungrammatical prepositional phrasing that Babel had popularized in *Red Cavalry*, e.g., "The Letter."

† Lavrenti Pavlovich Beria (1899–1953), close to Stalin, head of the NKVD (Soviet secret police) from 1939 to 1952.

General Procurator Rudenko had also brought out details of this crime during a 1956 trial in Tbilisi. On December 31, 1936, Nestor was given a state funeral and buried at the entrance to the Botanical Garden. Sometime after, however, he was declared an enemy of the people, so his body was exhumed and destroyed. All of Lakoba's close kin were executed.

※

FROM GAGRY WE MOVED ON BY CAR to Sukhumi where we spent several days. There, by the sea, Abram Room, the film director, was shooting a film starring Olga Zhizneva. In the mornings we went to the local market and in the afternoons we went to the famous Sukhumi monkey farm or else we would go down to the beach. Be it at the market or in special stands on the main street, *shashlik* was being grilled everywhere. Sukhumi was filled with the smell of roasted lamb. In the evenings people would meet at tea houses that served strong tea and bagels.

From Sukhumi we went by steamer to Tuapse, and from there we left by train for Kabardino-Balkariya. To get to our destination, the city of Nalchik, we had to change trains at Prokhladnaya. The train we needed arrived late at night when everyone was sleeping and was to leave for Nalchik in the morning. We left our things at the station and, unencumbered, we walked the local streets until we found a comfortable bench under a tree where we sat through the night.

The night was warm, and the moon was bright, its light turning the poplars all silver. There was the smell of dust and cows in the air. At sunrise we went off to the market.

"The market is the face of a city or village," Babel told me. "From the market and what is sold there, I can always tell what a city and its people are like. I love markets, and whenever I come to a town it's the first place I go."

When we arrived at the market, there were many horses and it was already full of people trading in livestock and grain. All the fowl being sold was alive. We bought warm flatcakes and cornbread dumplings, and then headed back to the station.

"The bounty of the past is gone — it is due to the famine in Ukraine and the destruction of the village across our land," Babel said.

A few hours later we reached Nalchik, where we checked into a hotel and ordered tea. I decided to try to get some sleep while Babel went off to see Betal Kalmykov, the First Secretary of the Regional Party.

Babel woke me up. He came into my room, laughing, and said: "Do you realize how long you've slept? It's already morning of the next day. Betal has invited us to move into his country home in Dolinskoe where he is staying now."

But I became intransigent. "I don't know Betal, so I cannot accept his invitation. You're the one he's inviting, not me, so I don't want to move in there. I don't want to, and that's that."

Babel's assurance that I would have my own room and that Betal regularly had all kinds of visitors, including Moscow correspondents and their wives, didn't matter to me. He could do nothing to sway me. He had to return to Party headquarters, where it was decided that he would move in with Betal while I would rent accommodations at a vacation home just across from Betal's residence. That I could accept, so we moved out to Dolinskoe. On the way there Babel told me about his meeting with Betal Kalmykov during our first day in Nalchik — the one I had slept through.

"I met Betal at the square where he was standing in front of the new State Planning Building. I went up to him and said:

'Beautiful building, Betal.' He replied, 'The building may be beautiful, but the people inside are no good. Let's go in.' We entered and I was surprised to hear him tell some woman that he wanted to go into the restroom, and could she make sure that it was empty. He invited me along. The restroom was no worse than what you'd find in any public institution in Moscow. But Betal was not satisfied. From the restroom he went to the director and when this man stood up to greet us, Betal said, without any preliminaries, 'You, sir, are a savage, a man of no culture whatsoever (*nekul'turnyi*). Your restroom is dirty.'"

In Dolinskoe Babel introduced me to Betal and his family. Betal Kalmykov was tall, broad-shouldered, and a bit stout, with slanted brown eyes and prominent cheekbones. He usually dressed in a gray jacket made of simple cloth called "devil's skin," and the matching pants were flared riding breeches; his shirt was bound by a narrow belt and its wrap-around collar was buttoned at the top. He wore fine kidskin boots and a *kubanka* — a brown Persian wool hat with a flat leather crown. He almost always wore his *kubanka*, even when at the table, and once, when he didn't have it on, I saw that he was bald. So I assume he was self-conscious about his baldness.

Betal's wife, Antonina Aleksandrovna, was a beautiful, robust Russian woman who, I believe, worked in child-care and public education. The Kalmykovs themselves had two children, Volodya who was then about twelve and Svetlana (Lana), who was three or four. Volodya was a handsome lad with Russian features, whereas Lana, her father's favorite, had Betal's prominent cheekbones and slanted, cunning eyes.

"Our daughter is going to be ugly — nobody will run off with her," said Betal, as he held her on his knees.

"She herself will run off with whomever she pleases," Babel answered with a laugh.

Mornings in Dolinskoe, Babel would either write or, more often, go somewhere with Betal. After lunch Babel would come by and during our walks together he would tell me about Betal or what he had heard from Betal over breakfast or lunch. I can recall some of what he told me.

"The Whites were after me" (so went one of his stories), "and I was fleeing into the mountains, taking familiar paths. They almost had me, but I got away. Still, I couldn't stop, for they kept coming — they had decided to track me down and kill me like a wild beast. My strength kept ebbing away — I didn't eat or sleep. It was all over after three days. I was so exhausted that I fell over, and when I rose, I found myself face to face with a buffalo. He was quivering, his eyes were watery. The buffalo was crying. It was breathing hard and, just like me, it couldn't take another step. The Whites had been hunting me down, and I, without knowing it, had been doing the same thing to the buffalo. And there we were facing each other, looking each other right in the eye. That was the first time I saw a buffalo cry."

In Kabardino-Balkariya a fairly large forested area was set aside as a reserve for bear, elk, boar and fowl of all kinds. Hunting was important to the people of Kabardino-Balkariya and Betal himself was a passionate hunter. More often than not his after-dinner stories had to do with hunting.

Occasionally government leaders from Moscow would come to the area to hunt. Once Marshall Voroshilov turned up at the head of a large hunting party. Babel told me what one of Betal's comrades had to say about this event.

"They were using shotguns. During the hunt one of the more inept visitors discharged a full load of shot into Betal's stomach. Betal didn't even let on he'd been hit and saw that the hunt went on to the very end. After the hunt they roasted fowl for dinner and only when all the guests had gone to bed did Betal lift his shirt and, using the light from the campfire and a pocketknife, he and his comrades removed over twenty pieces of lead from deep within his belly. Two inaccessible pieces remained. Nothing was said and the next day they went hunting for boar. Only after he'd seen his guests off did Betal seek medical help."

"What laws of hospitality they have here!" Babel remarked.

On another hunt, one of the guests shot Betal in the leg — the bullet hitting the bone. The next day he was scheduled to attend a meeting in Moscow. With difficulty he pulled his boot on and limped to the railway car. Once inside, the leg began to swell, so the boot had to be cut away. In Rostov, he was taken off the train and taken immediately to the hospital. Refusing categorically to lie on a stretcher, Betal walked on his own to the car and then to the operating table. They wanted to tie his arms and legs to the table, but he resisted this and steadfastly refused to be given any anesthesia. "In the Caucasus we don't like violence against the individual, so don't you touch me. I'm not going to scream — I just want to see the operation for myself."

"For the first time in my life," Betal related, "I saw a human bone. What a beautiful thing! Pearly white with pink and blue striations. I saw the doctor remove the bullet and sew my skin up. Having finished the operation, the doctor said, 'Well, Comrade Kalmykov, everything's all right, but your bear-hunting days are over.' I replied: 'Not at all, doctor, and I'll send you the skin of the first bear I kill.' I was in bed for over a month, then I began to walk, but it wasn't easy, my knee wouldn't bend. I thought and thought and then decided to dip my leg in hot water and try to bend it slowly. I did this every day. At first it was very painful, but *now* look!" Betal shook his leg which easily bent at the knee. "I sent the doctor in Rostov the skin of the first bear I shot."

In 1933 Kabardino-Balkariya was a region of what seemed to be unimaginable plenty. The markets were overflowing with goods, the horses well-fed, the cows and sheep nicely fatted.

From Nalchik, Babel wrote his mother: "I've been making the rounds of the Kabardino-Balkariya region — a diamond among Soviet regions. I can't say how happy I am to have come here. Not only is the harvest enormous, but it's been brought in splendidly. How pleasant, at last, to live in our Russian bounty."

When it was time to harvest the corn Betal insisted that all the Nalchik regional party and state workers help. Betal himself, together with his wife, Antonina Aleksandrovna, headed out to the fields. They worked for days on end and Betal led everyone — indeed his average harvest exceeded that of the most seasoned *kolkhoz* worker.

"In every respect this man is number one in Kabardino-Balkariya," Babel said. "He's the best hunter, no one can match him. He is the best harvester of corn, nobody can compete with him in this skill, and he is the best rider, the most skilled person overall... Betal is surrounded by the comrade-partisans with whom, in the past, he had fought against the Whites. I found this out for myself. Last night we were walking through the park together, and the pathways were covered with fallen leaves. Suddenly Betal said, addressing no one in particular, 'The walkways need sweeping.' And close by from out of the darkness someone said: 'It shall be done.' He's always surrounded by his personal security guard made up of comrades from the partisan days," Babel repeated. "And when Stalin took measures to see that Betal had an official security force and bodyguards to accompany him everywhere, Betal could hardly stand it, and he mocked them mercilessly. Not long ago I accompanied Betal to see an electric power station that was under construction. We got out of the car and began walking along a path. Two Red Army soldiers got out of the next car and set off behind us. Suddenly, we saw a coiled snake on the path right in front of us. Betal turned around and said to one of the bodyguards: 'So, kill the snake!' The bodyguard stopped dead in his tracks, totally at a loss as to how to approach the snake. Betal strode forward, bent over, took hold of the snake in some special way, and threw it on the ground. It was dead. Turning around, he said ironically: 'How are you going to defend me when you're afraid to kill a snake?' And Betal walked on."

The power station under construction was Betal Kalmykov's pride and joy. He spoke about it frequently and went to the construction site almost daily.

Babel attended a special regional meeting for communist instructors who had been sent to Balkariya by Moscow to liquidate the remaining private farm holdings — some fifteen percent overall. Babel recounted Betal's speech to these instructors.

"Throw down your noisy popguns — there's no war out here. Go live with people in the pastures, sleep with them in their huts, eat the same food they do, and remember that you are not going off to regulate someone else's life — but your very own. I'll be right on your heels. I know you will find people who will say that everything is fine, but . . . some oldster will step forward and tell me the truth. If you manage to make everything go right, how good you will feel about celebrating the anniversary of the Revolution. If you make a mess of things, I'll *testroy* you, *testroy* each and every one of you.'"

"This was not to be taken lightly, and the instructors turned pale," said Babel as he finished his story.

❋

I WAS GROWING WEARY of indolence and, once, when I saw some women harvesting carrots, I joined them and worked until lunch. My mood immediately picked up and I had a good appetite for the first time since arriving in Nalchik. I didn't say anything about this work to Babel when he came by after lunch, but Betal had already told him.

"That man knows everything going on in his realm at each and every moment. He cannot have it otherwise," Babel said.

We soon had further confirmation of this. At the end of October Betal proposed that we go to a unique vantage point from which the entire crest of the Caucasus Mountains could be seen, including a simultaneous view of Mount Elbrus and Mount Kazbek. On a sunny morning Babel and I left on horseback. On our way to the promontory, riders sent by Betal twice overtook us to make sure that everything was all right.

We decided to go back to Nalchik the following evening, but first we wanted to spend the night on Mount Nartukh so that we could see the mountains at dawn. I had never before seen alpine meadows; high above sea level, on a slightly hilly expanse, a green carpet with flowers and haystacks spread out before us. It was extremely hot. One could hardly imagine that back in Moscow the trees were standing naked under a cold rain. That night we all sat around a fire where fresh ears of corn were cooked in a big pot. From time to time we heard around us the din and clamor of the night watchmen. They were busy driving away the bears who were trying to steal the harvest.

Finally, the mountains began to emerge from the pre-dawn haze. At first they were somber, dark blue and violet, but then, here and there, they started glowing pink as though someone

With father, 1902.

had set them on fire. Then everything exploded into hues of every sort — the sun had risen. Spread out before us was the whole expanse of the Caucasus Mountains. To our left — Kazbek; to the right Elbrus; and between them, chains of mountain summits.

Babel went off with some hunters to an elevated blind from which they could watch the boar as they came down to drink from a watering hole. In a letter to his mother Babel wrote about this:

"I went hunting for boar with Evdokimov and Kalmykov. We got a few (with no help from me, of course) and we roasted them whole at an altitude of 2,000 meters with a view of the entire Caucasus chain from Novorossisk to Baku."

I myself didn't see Betal that day, but he had probably come to hunt in the morning before returning to Nalchik. We stayed up on Mount Nartukh until midday and did not return to Dolinskoe until that evening.

Sometime afterwards we went with Betal to see the Baksanskoe Gorge at the foot of Mount Elbrus. The sun was hot and water from melting glacial snow flowed in many rivulets into the little Baksan river. Babel smiled as he recounted, "Betal got fed up with reading newspaper accounts of heroic alpinists climbing to the top of Mount Elbrus. He decided to debunk once and for all the legend about the incredible difficulties of the climb. He assembled 500 ordinary collective farmers and, with no special gear, they climbed to the very summit. Today, when he is asked about this, he just chuckles."

While at the Baksanskoe Gorge we spent several days living in Betal's green cottage, not far from the local Balkar settlement. During our walks we would frequently come across bubbling narzan mineral springs, which we would recognize by the iron tinges in the surrounding earth.

At that time Babel wrote to his mother: "We spent several days at a Balkar settlement in the foothills of Mount Elbrus. It was 3,000 meters high, and on the first day I had some difficulty breathing, then got used to it. "

Babel traveled with Betal to visit the Balkar settlements. He used to come back tired, yet full of the most varied impressions. "What people these are! Every shepherd has so much dignity! And how they all believe in Betal! As for him, all his thoughts are focused on the well-being of his people."

From the Baksanskoe Gorge we planned to ride to the Adyl-Su pass so that we could look out over the sea from there. But the day before we were to go a blizzard came over the mountains and we had to return to Nalchik.

The anniversary of the Revolution arrived. Beginning early in the morning equestrian events with prizes were held not far from Nalchik. The official guests invited from Moscow were seated in wooden stands specially erected for the occasion. During the races a miserably dressed woman with a child in her arms came up to Betal in the stands and said a few words to him in Kabardinian. Betal turned quickly to the President of the Regional Executive and asked in Russian, "Is she with the *kolkhoz*?"

"They're shiftless," came the reply.

Betal said something to the woman, who got down off the stands and left. Betal had been in good spirits, but now he had turned somber. Babel asked his neighbor, "What did the woman say?"

His neighbor translated: "Betal, we belong to the *kolkhoz* and we are starving. As payment for days worked we got ten kilograms of sunflower seed. My husband is ill and we have nothing to eat."

"And what did Betal say?" Babel asked.

"He said he'd go see them tomorrow."

Once the races were over and the prizes awarded we went to the parking lot and Betal opened the door to one of the cars and invited me to take a seat. His wife, Antonina Aleksandrovna, sat beside me. Babel and Betal got into another car and they started off in front of us. Since we were traveling over a dusty country road, I asked the driver if we couldn't pass them.

His response was blunt, "That's not the way it's done here."

Perplexed, I looked at Antonina Aleksandrovna, who smiled and said, "I've grown used to it."

In the evening we went to a holiday concert. A dancer dressed in national costume and wearing leather boots as soft as women's stockings came out and danced the *lezginka*, and with exceptional virtuosity started dropping to one knee. Betal, who was sitting in the first row, suddenly became outraged and stood up and berated the dancer for his invention and for breaking with his father's customs. After the concert Babel whispered to me, "See, his guardianship even covers the *lezginka*!"

The next day Betal kept his word to the woman with the baby and went to see her in the settlement where she lived. Babel went with him and, quite shaken, he returned and gave this account: "On the way to the settlement we stopped off to pick up the district Party Secretary and the President of the *kolkhoz*. Just the way Betal opened the car door for them and, bowing, invited them to take a seat, caused them to go cold. As we drove to the woman's home, Betal said: 'Has the good life so hardened your hearts? This woman came to see every last one of you before coming up to see me.' And then later he added: 'What's the difference between you people and me? You cross a bridge, see a drowning child, and drive right on. Me, I'll stop and save the child. Has the good life so hardened your hearts?'

"But the district secretary and President kept to their line:

'These people are shiftless. They don't want to work.'

"We drove up to a little peasant hut, walked through a weed-infested courtyard, and entered the hut. The woman's husband, dressed in rags, was in bed and going through agony" — *going through agony* — these were Babel's very words.

"The room was neat, though nearly empty. On the table there was a bag of sunflower seeds. The woman with the baby was not home. Betal looked around carefully and spoke a bit with the *kolkhoznik* — had he been sick for very long, how many workdays had his family accumulated, what sort of advance had he gotten for them. . . Then, turning to the district secretary, he said: 'I'm calling a meeting of the Regional Committee for the day after tomorrow, and it's going to be held in this man's yard. By that time, you are to build a new home for this man, you are to see that he and his family receive the food they need and that they are paid in full for the work they've done.' Then, after having gone out into the yard, he added: 'You will see that all the weeds are cut down and,' with a gesture toward a corner of the yard, 'you will have an outhouse put in over there.' Then Betal got into the car and we left," Babel said, ending his story.

The day for the meeting that Betal had called was changed, but still the amount of time allowed for building the house was so small that we were all excited about the outcome. So many people wanted to attend the meeting that I felt I could not ask Babel to take me with him. I was anxious to hear what he had to say when he returned.

"When we arrived there stood a new house — completely finished except for masonry work on the oven. The weeds had been cut down and we could see the outhouse in the far corner. Not only was the entire yard full of people, but the adjacent streets and garden patches as well. Betal had taken such a liking to the words he'd said earlier to the district secretary and the *kolkhoz* President that he repeated them in his Russian speech to the members of the Regional Committee. 'Has the good life so hardened your hearts?' Then he spoke in Kabardinian. I grabbed the nearest person to me by the sleeve and asked, 'What's he saying?' The man looked back and said, 'He's reamin' out someun.' Betal's voice had an edge to it and his eyes were flashing, so, after a while, I again asked my neighbor, 'What's he saying now?' 'He's reamin' us all out,' the man said, turning his scared face toward me. And finally, as Betal started to yell and I thought he would end up with the standard 'Long live Stalin,' I again asked my neighbor: 'Now, what's he saying?' 'He says we've got to build more outhouses.' That's how Betal finished his speech."

Babel had more stories about Betal. I remember the following one.

"Betal assembled the girls from Kabardino-Balkariya and told them, 'Horses and cows can be sold, but not young women. Don't let your parents sell you. You should marry for love.' One girl stood up and said, 'We don't agree. Why do you think we should be given away free? Our parents need the income. No, we cannot agree.' Betal got angry and called together the young men. 'Go off to Ukraine and choose your brides there; Ukrainian girls are much better — they're big-breasted and good at keeping house.' So he sent the lads off to the nearest Ukrainian settlements to get their wives. Then, the young women sent a delegation to see Betal to declare, 'We agree.' "

※

BABEL WROTE HIS MOTHER about a conference for elderly people that Betal had called: "Tomorrow, there is a regional conference for elderly men and women. They are the prime movers behind kolkhoz construction. They oversee everything, they show young people what to do, they wear badges that say 'Quality Inspector,' and, in general, are highly regarded. Conferences like these, with music playing and applause for the elderly, are now being held all over the land. The person who first initiated this is Kalmykov, First Secretary of the Regional Party Committee — with whom I am currently staying. By birth he's a Kabardinian, but, in essence, he's a new man, a great man of the sort we haven't seen before. His renown has been spreading for some fifteen years, but the reality far outstrips the rumors one hears about him. By sheer determination and vision he's turning a small, semi-savage alpine land into a real gem."

Betal was one of the people who captured Babel's imagination. Sometimes, he would grow pensive and say, "I want to understand: Betal, what is he?"

Another time, as Babel was pacing his room, he said, "Betal's relations with Moscow are complicated. When Moscow sends its Central Committee plenipotentiaries here they stay in a special railway car and ask Betal to come see them. He goes in and sits by the door on the edge of his seat. This he does on purpose. Once they asked him, 'Is it true, Comrade Betal, that gold has been discovered in the sand of the Nalchik River?' He replied: 'For the present that's not something we talk about.' He acts like a nobody and demeans himself, yet he's a proud man, and I don't think he respects them all that much. In this regard, Moscow fully reciprocates. He's been given very little in money and products. Yet, without Moscow knowing about it, he's covered his country with a network of beautifully paved roads. I asked him once where he got the money for this. It turns out that he'd appealed to his people to gather the fruit that grows abundantly in the wild here, pears and apples, and he built factories to process the fruit into jam and jelly. The proceeds are used for the construction of roads. Incidentally, we have been invited to visit one of these factories..."

And this we did. Betal himself took us along with some other guests, and showed us the processing equipment. His favorite expression for praising someone was, "A worker and a decent sort." And for criticizing someone, "A savage, a person of no culture." At the jam factory he did not criticize anyone; indeed, on a few occasions he used the term "a worker and a decent sort."

Betal offered jars of jam and jelly to all the guests. Many accepted, but Babel and I refused the offer. Later, Babel told me, "Betal speaks very highly of you — probably because you refused his jelly." Here, Babel started laughing. "But maybe it's because you lead such an independent life here. He's even about to ask you to work as an engineer on the construction of a hydroelectric station. Would you say yes?"

"No, I wouldn't," I answered. "I'm planning to work as a designer on the Moscow subway."

In the winter, or possibly the spring, of 1934, when Babel was back in Moscow, he learned that in the northern Caucasus sports competitions held in Piatigorsk, the Kaberdinians and Balkarians placed first in every event. Bearing this news, Babel came to see me in my room and said: "Among the peoples of the northern Caucasus, neither the Kabardinians nor the Balkarians are distinguished by their physical strength, yet they took first place in *every* event. When he was seeing his athletes off, I wonder what Betal said to them. I'd give a lot to know."

In February of 1935 Babel wrote to his mother: "The Congress of Soviets is being held in Moscow; friends arrived from all over — Evdokimov came from the northern Caucasus,

Kalmykov from Kabardino-Balkariya, and there were many friends from the Donbass. I'm spending a lot of time with them and get to bed around four or five in the morning. Last night Kalmykov and I took Kabardinian dancers to Gorky's home. Their dancing was unforgettable."

Some time after, I think in 1936, Betal again came to Moscow and Babel said to me, "Go see Betal at his hotel and persuade him to see a doctor. I know he's sick; in all likelihood he's got a stomach ulcer, yet he won't see a doctor. Maybe he'll listen to you. And, by the way, pick up some oranges for Lana."

So, carrying a bag of oranges, I went off to visit Betal. I found him sitting on the couch in his hotel room, still wearing his hat of lamb's wool, and eating fried eggs right out of the skillet. He greeted me with a smile. After we had exchanged the usual niceties, I purposely used his favorite expression and said, "Betal, you are a savage, a person of no culture — why won't you consult a doctor about your illness?"

He laughed and said, "My illness is a fiction — I'm completely healthy." And on that note my admonitions ended.

Some time afterwards, most likely in 1937, Babel told me about Betal's arrest: "He was summoned to Moscow for a meeting with the Central Committee, and as he was walking into a room four or five men jumped him. Given his strength, they had decided not to risk a standard arrest. They disarmed him and bound him — this Betal, who could endure anything except violence directed against him! After Betal's arrest the Kabardino-Balkariya party leaders were summoned to a meeting. The train that brought representatives of the Central Committee to Nalchik was filled with NKVD military guards. These armed guards formed two rows that stretched from the train station to the building where the party leaders had gathered. The party leaders were informed that Betal Kalmykov was an enemy of the people and that he had been arrested. After the meeting, all the leaders were marched to the train down a path formed by the soldiers and hauled off to Moscow prisons."

Betal perished.

And so it was that Babel's cycle of tales about Kabardino-Balkariya remained unwritten.

❋

ONCE HE HAD FINISHED visiting Nalchik, Babel made plans to go off to a *kolkhoz* in the Prishibskaya settlement where he wanted to gather material and write. He decided to see me off to Moscow and, on the way, show me the "Mineral Group." For a while we stayed in Zheleznovodsk. Not far from there was the Tersky stud farm, which greatly interested Babel.

On our way there, Babel told me: "The Tersky stud farm has been around for several years. It was set up for the specific reason of getting offspring from Cylinder, a remarkable Arabian stallion. The problem is, though, that Cylinder has only sired females. No matter what mare they give him, they can't come up with a male ... "

At the stud farm they showed us Cylinder. I had never in all my life seen a more beautiful horse. Except for his silver mane and tail he was white all over, and his neck was arched just like a swan's. At the stud farm near Molodenovo and at the Moscow Racetrack Babel had already managed to show me some first-rate thoroughbreds, but those had just been trotters. This was the first time I had seen an Arabian pure-blood. Until then I hadn't believed such beautiful creatures existed.

"Well, what do you think?" Babel asked. "Worth a stud farm, wasn't he?"

We spent nearly a whole day at the stud farm. They led

Cylinder's line before us — two-year-olds and three-year-olds. Not one of these mares had even inherited his coloring.

In Pyatigorsk, Babel showed me all of the places connected with Lermontov. Babel had been there before to visit his "fellow soldiers," as he referred to the comrades he had met in 1920 while serving in the Red Cavalry. As a result, Babel showed me around with all the expertise of a real tour guide.

"Our country is simply not yet ready for tourism," he said. "The hotels are terrible; the rooms are furnished with bare tables and with beds of poor quality covered by miserable gray blankets."

From Kislovodsk Babel took me to the railway station at Mineralnye Vody where I departed. Shortly after my return to Moscow I received a letter from Babel postmarked Prishibskaya. I remember the following lines very well: "I'm living in a mud hut with an earthen floor. I'm toiling away. Yesterday evening, as night fell, I was sitting with the *kolkhoz* chairman and he yelled out: "Hey, Fyodor, go supervise a lamp for us.""

And just before the New Year's holiday I received a letter in which Babel wrote, "I'm a superstitious man, and absolutely must celebrate New Year's with you. Don't start working just yet and come to Gorlovka on the 31st. I'll be there to meet you."

Babel's invitation carried with it a proposal that we live together from then on. My coming to Gorlovka on December 31, 1933 meant that I had accepted.

Babel was waiting for me in a lined sheepskin coat, a fur hat, and felt boots. He took me to see Venyamin Yakovlevich Furer, the secretary of the Gorlovka City Council, at whose home we stayed.

Furer was famous and much had been written about him. His fame was due to his having created, by the standards of that time, excellent living conditions for miners. He had even had rose bushes planted along the walkway from their living quarters to the mine. Furer gave honor and respect to grueling, dirty work. Miners were a privileged group at the local workers' club, were regularly praised, and given awards and bonuses. This raised their status as grooms, so the very best young women were happy to marry them.

Babel and I joined Furer in the New Year's festivities. Furer's wife, the Kharkov ballerina Galina Lerkh, was unable to join us. Furer's Gorlovka apartment was large but nearly empty, and its simple furniture was limited to the bare essentials. His household was run by a very spunky, freckle-faced girl with a cheerful disposition and a sharp tongue. She said just what she thought to Furer and even bossed him around, while for his part, he found it amusing to let her take over, saying, "She's loyal, and, strange as it may seem, she helps me in my work by keeping me from becoming a bureaucrat."

Furer was a very handsome man — tall, well-built, and blond with bright, merry blue eyes. "One of nature's finest creations," Babel said of him.

Over New Year's dinner Furer joked about being besieged by reporters who wrote incredible rubbish about him. One of them, after visiting his parents, had written, "The elderly Furers had given birth to the curly-headed boy." Babel found that phrasing amusing and often repeated it.

While in Gorlovka Babel wanted to go down into the mine to observe the miners at work. We were accompanied by the writer Zozulya, who was also visiting Gorlovka. In the showers we changed into miners clothing and each of us was given a lamp that we strapped around our chests. Outfitted in this way, and accompanied by a shift foreman and an engineer, we made a quick descent by elevator to a thick vein of coal being worked along a steep 70° gradient.

After the engineer lowered himself into a narrow opening, I went next, followed by the foreman, Babel and Zozulya. We had to descend in darkness broken only by the fairly murky light of the lamps we were wearing. The air was full of coal dust that immediately clogged one's eyes, nose, and mouth.

The supporting timbers where the vein had already been worked were about 1.5–1.7 meters apart, so I found the descent to be very difficult. One had to maintain a spread-eagled position from which it was essential to stretch out to the very utmost. Meanwhile, one could hardly see anything and there was absolutely no air to breathe. One's hands and feet quickly went numb while one's heart pounded full-force. For my part, I felt such despair that I was ready to let go and plummet down. The engineer who had gone first was able to help me, however; from time to time he'd simply grab my leg and place it on the next timber, so it was hardly by my own will that I let go of the timbers above me. I had reached a point of near despair when, suddenly, I felt the vein of coal against my back, and this provided some relief. If one descended on one's back it was much easier, but nobody had told us this. I was concerned about Babel — he was just slightly taller than I and, in addition, suffered from asthma — so I asked the foreman to help him and to tell him that he should use his back for support.

To the right of us we saw miners hacking coal — their cursing went beyond anything imaginable. This was all part of tradition — no cursing, no coal. In one spot we drew closer to the area where they were working. The coal glowed and sparkled by the light of the lamps. It was real anthracite.

Babel was not talking with the miners — clearly, it was too difficult for him to talk. I looked at him and saw that, like everyone else, his face was totally black except for the whites of his eyes and his teeth. He was finding it difficult to breathe.

We began to descend further. It seemed to get easier, maybe because the vein sloped more gently. For the last few meters we simply slid on our backs into a pile of coal and nearly tumbled into a coal trolley. After yet another descent along a ladder fixed to the wall of the mine, we reached a fairly large drift-away, where the ceiling and walls had been whitewashed and the air was clean. The foreman repeatedly warned the miners: "Quiet, there's a woman here." But no matter how hard he tried, the profanity never stopped. When one jolly young fellow saw that visitors had come, he bawled out: "For some real pretty cussing you should go to the pump room." Babel called back, "The men in the pump room are more educated, that's why their swearing is more exquisite!"

Babel found that the swearing in the pump room had fully lost any direct meaning and had turned into pure form, although as form it did possess a certain virtuosity and poetic quality. In the pump room they swore in verses adapted from Pushkin and Esenin; one could actually distinguish the meters and styles.

We climbed up to the surface and went to the showers to wash. The water there was special, a concentrate derived from steam, and it washed the coal off very well, though we were all left with dark circles around the eyes that did not wash off for several days.

Babel's face was calm and his appearance gave no sign that he had just had to cross the very coals of hell. Inquisitive about everything, he asked the engineer a number of questions.

❋

FURER LEFT FOR TWO DAYS to visit his wife in Kharkov. When he returned he spoke passionately about his plans for

Babel in his mid-twenties.

transforming Gorlovka — a hospital going in here, a city park there, and across the way, a theater. He also dreamed of reducing the workday for miners to four hours.

On January 20, 1934 Babel wrote his mother from Gorlovka: "Visiting the Donbass was absolutely the right thing to do. It is a region essential to know. Sometimes I fall into despair — how to master artistically this boundless, nonstop, unprecedented land we call the USSR. The spirit of confidence and success is greater now than at any time in these 16 years of revolution."

Furer was never able to realize his plans for Gorlovka. Kaganovich* summoned him to Moscow to work in the Party Committee.

But in 1934, Babel, Furer, Galina Lerkhi, and I went to Tushino to attend a parade devoted to Soviet aviation. As we were driving along a side street in order to avoid the crush of traffic heading into Tushino we noticed a warehouse sign that read: "Absolutely no sand-taking." This prompted Babel to remember a number of similarly odd signs, and a particular one he had once seen in the Crimea: "Hacking Christmas trees from firs is strictly forbidden."

We watched the parade from the top of an administration building, where many famous people had gathered. Next to us stood A. N. Tupolev,† then at the peak of his fame, his reputation later to be almost extinguished. Stalin and other members of the government stood at the very front.

Some time later, when we were invited to attend one of Lerkhi's performances, we again met Furer. As I recall, the performance was held at some club on Razin Street. The auditorium

---

*Lazar Moiseyevich Kaganovich (1893–1991), secretary of the Central Committee of the Communist Party and close to Stalin.

† Andrei Nikolaevich Tupolev (1888–1972), Soviet aircraft designer.

was not very large, but it was packed. Lerkhi's "character dances" were very expressive and seemed quite modern when compared to classical ballet. Babel said that her dance numbers were "in the style of Isadora Duncan," whom he had known.

I saw Furer for the last time in the fall of 1936. Shortly before our meeting, Babel went to Odessa, and, during his absence, I decided that he should no longer be living in the same apartment with foreigners. So I called Furer and told him that I needed to speak with him right away. He invited me over that evening. The same spunky, freckle-faced girl from Gorlovka opened the door when I arrived.

I found Furer seated at the desk in his study. The purpose of my visit was to explain that, given the trials of the "enemies of the people" then going on, it was hardly wise for Babel to be living with foreigners. In short, Babel needed a separate apartment. Had he been present, Babel almost certainly would have ridiculed my thinking. Still, Furer fully agreed with me and promised to give some thought to the apartment. I noticed that all of his desk drawers were pulled out and that, while listening to me, Furer was removing letters and some papers and ripping them to shreds. A mound of shredded paper sat on his desk. I didn't pay much attention to this at the time, for I simply assumed he was cleaning out his desk.

But shortly afterwards, Babel wrote me from Odessa: "Today, I learned that F is dead. How terrible!" I wracked my brains for a long time trying to figure out who among our acquaintances had a name starting with "F" — but with no result. Furer's name never crossed my mind, for I simply could not imagine that someone in power, and as close to the very fortunate Kaganovich, could experience misfortune.

When word of Furer's death finally got through to me I realized that I had been talking to him on the eve of his suicide. We had met on a Saturday evening, and on Sunday he had gone to his dacha and shot himself. Later on Babel told me that Stalin was very irritated by Furer's act, saying: "How childish it is to shoot yourself without saying anything first." As for me, I thought Furer was much too young to be a part of some oppositional faction. His record was spotless, he was highly regarded, so I could not begin to comprehend the threat of arrest he was facing. Back then I still naively believed that for someone to be arrested, there had to be a reason.

In any case, back in January of 1934, it had been a different Furer, a merry fellow full of hope, who had seen Babel and me off on the train to Moscow.

※

WHEN WE RETURNED TO MOSCOW, Shtainer met us at the Nikolo-Vorobinsky home and it was obvious that he already suspected his "gentlemen's agreement" with Babel — no women whatsoever on the premises — was about to be broken. We therefore decided to accustom him gradually and within a few days rented me a room at 3 Tverskaia-Yamskaya Street, in the three-room apartment of an engineer. Besides the engineer and his wife, a housekeeper named Ustya lived there. She was a cheerful person, not young, who loved to tell stories about the lives of her employers, and whenever she got going, it was impossible to drag Babel away. He was always especially amused by the way she answered me on the telephone. I would ask, "How are things at home?" She would say, "When we meet we'll talk."

Babel and I continued to live separately for a few months, until Shtainer himself suggested to Babel that I move into the

Nikolo-Vorobinsky home, and he gave me one of his two upstairs rooms, judging it to be more comfortable than Babel's
second room. Shortly after this, Babel gave away his second
room to a neighbor on the other side of the building, the door
was bricked over, and only three of the upstairs rooms remained
for us.

Babel's bedroom was also his workroom. It was a corner
room with big windows, furnished with a bed (eventually replaced by a settee), an armoire, two chairs, a small end table
with a drawer, bookcases, and a work table next to which stood
a little, hard-cushioned couch. Babel had ordered the bookcases
specially built to the height of the windowsills and extending
the length of the room. They contained the books he needed as
well as those he loved best. On top of the bookcases he would lay
out sheets of paper on which he wrote plans for stories, notes, or
rough drafts. He would cut these sheets himself so that they
were extra long, fifteen or sixteen by ten centimeters, and then
he would fill them completely with notations. He would either
work sitting on the little couch, often with his feet crossed under
him, or else walking back and forth across the room. He would
go from corner to corner with a piece of rough twine in his
hands, or a thin cord that he would keep winding and unwinding on his fingers. From time to time he would stop at the table
or at a bookcase and jot something down on one of the long
sheets. Then his pacing deliberations would start again. Sometimes he would even go beyond the confines of his room, wan-
der into mine, stand there a little while, still winding and
unwinding the string in silence, and then he would go back to
his room. Once an actual rosary appeared in Babel's hands, obtained from somewhere or other, and he fingered the beads as
he worked; but after about three days the rosary disappeared,
and he went back to winding string or unbleached yarn on his

fingers. Sitting cross-legged was something he could do for hours, and it seemed to me that this ability came from the way he was built.

Babel kept his manuscripts in the lower drawer of the armoire. Only his diaries and notebooks were locked up in a small, rather heavy metal box.

As for my looking at his manuscripts, Babel frightened me on that score from the very beginning, as soon as I moved in. He told me that I was not supposed to read anything written in rough draft, and that when something was ready, he himself would read it to me. I never disobeyed this rule. Now I have come to regret it. But Babel was so alert to all around him that I believed he could see through everything. He himself recounted that Gorky had said to him, laughing, "You are a born intelligence man. It's terrifying to let you in the door."

And even when Babel was not home, I was afraid of his penetrating eyes.

By that time I was already working for the "Metroproject," the engineering group that had been put in charge of planning the first line of the Moscow subway. Babel regarded my work with great respect as well as curiosity.

The construction of the Moscow subway went very fast. The planners were rushed to complete their work, and there were times when I had to bring work home, either to complete or check over construction calculations. Babel would always stop by my room to look things over, either leafing silently through a paper folder full of calculations or else carrying it off with him to his room. If he had a visitor there, such as a film director, he would show him the papers and boast: "This is a real mathematician we have here." Once I heard him say: "Just take a look at how complicated this stuff is, it's not like writing some scenario ..."

Designing and drawing blueprints, which I also had to do at home sometimes, seemed to be incomprehensible to Babel, whereas for me what was unfathomable was Babel's ability and the extent of his knowledge.

✻

BEFORE I MET BABEL I used to read a great deal, though without any particular direction. I read whatever I could get my hands on. Babel noticed this and told me, "Reading that way will get you nowhere. You won't have enough time to read the books that are truly worthwhile. There are about a hundred books that every educated person needs to read. Sometime I'll try to make you a list of them." And a few days later he brought me a list. There were ancient writers on it, Greek and Roman — Homer, Heroditus, Lucretius, Suetonius — and also all the classics of later Western European literature, starting with Erasmus, Rabelais, Cervantes, Swift, and Coster, and going on to nineteenth-century writers such as Stendhal, Mérimée, and Flaubert.

Once Babel brought me a book in two thick volumes, Faber's *The Instincts and Morals of Insects*. "I bought this for you in a second-hand bookstore," he said, "and even though I didn't put it on your list, it's something you have to read. You'll enjoy it."

And really, the book's style was so lively and engaging that it read like a detective novel.

Babel was always eager to show me something or to introduce me to someone. He would say: "You'll find this interesting" or "funny" or "useful."

Knowing that I could read some German, Babel pushed me to study classical German literature and even hired an instructor for me. With her help I read many many works by Lessing, Schiller, Goethe, and Heine, and I learned dozens of poems by heart.

Since Heine's prose was full of French words, Babel decided that I also needed to learn French. He arranged for a teacher to come from the Institute of Foreign Languages and I began lessons with her. I enjoyed them very much, but unfortunately they were not to last long and were over by the spring of 1939.

Babel's primary concern, in relation to me, seemed to be that I not feel deprived of youthful pleasures. He sought out companions who would invite me to go ice-skating, and he once found a group of skiers to take me off on Sundays to a dacha outside Moscow where I could ski in the forest. If a man came to visit him, Babel sometimes asked if he knew how to dance, and then would say, "Please dance with Antonina Nikolaevna, she loves to dance." He himself would turn on the record player and watch us dance with enjoyment.

In the summer of 1934 and for years afterwards I often went to the races with Babel, but I never saw him gambling. His interest in horses was strictly that of a sportsman. He spent much more time at training workouts or in the jockeys' stables than he spent at the races themselves. Racing amused him less, although the people he met at the races — especially the more ardent gamblers — interested him a great deal. At the track, whenever possible, he would eavesdrop on conversations avidly, always looking around with excited attention, and often he dragged me out of the box up to where the most zealous bettors sat. They would band together to purchase a single ticket that they had judged to be a sure winner.

I eventually learned how to tell when Babel was off visiting the horses by a foolproof domestic sign: if all the sugar was gone from the sugar bowl, it was a horse day.

Babel seldom went to the theater, venturing there only with great caution, but he did go every season to see the Moscow Art Theater's production of *Dead Souls.** He always laughed so hard during these performances that I would be embarrassed to be sitting next to him. To my knowledge it was the play that Babel liked best.

Once Babel went to the Moscow Art Theater when his play *Mariya* was being given its first reading, and when he returned home he told me that all the actresses had been impatient to find out what the leading female role was like and who would be cast in it. It turned out that there was no leading female character present on the stage in this play. Babel thought the play had not come off well, but it should be noted that he was always critical of his own work.

Babel liked neither operas nor operettas, but he loved listening to song recitals, especially when they were performed in small recital halls. He once came home ecstatic over a performance by a singer named Keto Dzhaparidze.

"This woman," he told me, "used to be the wife of one of the most powerful Party bosses in Georgia and used to sing only at home, for guests. Then her husband was arrested, and she found herself with no means of support at all. A friend advised her to sing professionally, which she did. She tried performing in a club and was met with incredible appreciation. After that she became a concert artist. She sings with unusually high emotion." The next time Keto Dzhaparidze gave a concert in Moscow Babel took me to hear her.

---

* Mikhail Bulgakov's dramatization of Gogol's classic novel.

※

ONCE I CAME HOME from the theater and found the apartment full of visitors. They were all journalists, among whom I knew only V. A. Reginin. I could see that Babel, his back to the wall, was pale with exhaustion as the journalists besieged him with questions. I gathered all my courage, went up to them and said, "Don't you know that Babel dislikes literary discussions?"

They stepped back and Reginin said: "Well, we'll talk another time."

And everyone left. Then Babel said to me: "Go wash your feet, I'll drink the bathwater."

Babel's dislike of literary questions bordered on absolute intolerance. M. Y. Makotinsky's daughter, Valentina Mikhailovna, told me an anecdote from the past that touches on this. The poet Vera Inber once tried — it would have been around 1927–1928 — to interview Babel, and she asked him about his literary plans for the year ahead. His answer, "Well, I am seriously thinking about buying a goat."

※

BABEL WAS ALWAYS DRAWN to the cinema. Once when he and I went to the Taganka Theater to see the film *Chapaev*, he left the theater shaken and said, "What a remarkable film! I should also add that I'm a remarkable viewer and that filmmakers should pay me to see their work. I can always judge correctly, afterwards, if the film was well-acted or well-made, but while I'm watching it I experience a film totally, to the exclusion of all else. A viewer like that is priceless."

IN THE SUMMER OF 1934, the French writer André Malraux arrived from Paris on his first visit to Moscow. Quite tall and a little stoop-shouldered, he was a very elegant man whose large and serious eyes on his thin face commanded one's attention. A nervous tic constantly played across his face. He had dark blond hair combed back smooth except for one lock that fell on his forehead, which he was always tossing back with a gesture of his head.

All three of us — Malraux, Babel, and I — went to see a sports parade on Red Square. We were seated in the tribunal for foreign guests. I spotted the writer H. G. Wells standing not far from us. As I had my camera with me, I suddenly took it into my head to get a photograph of Wells. Moving closer to where he stood while looking through the camera, I accidentally stepped on the foot of the Japanese ambassador and became terribly flustered. Babel noticed what had happened and he hurriedly joined us to smooth things over. He asked the ambassador with a smile, "So tell me, is it true that in Japan for reproduction you only need a bud?"

The ambassador laughed, made a joke in reply, and the whole matter was dropped. To me though, Babel said softly, "You almost caused an incident with the Japanese government. Be a little more careful when you are walking around ambassadors."

I did not try to take any more photographs. The tribunal for foreign guests was near Lenin's Mausoleum, on top of which Stalin stood, clearly visible in profile. After the parade we walked over to the Hotel Nationale to have dinner in the restaurant. All during the meal Malraux kept asking me about the role of love in the lives of Soviet women, how they looked upon adultery, how they felt about virginity, and so on. I answered as best I could. Babel translated my answers into French and doubtless made them wittier. In any case, Malraux, looking his most serious, kept nodding his head.

At some point during that first visit Malraux said, "Being a writer is not a profession." He was surprised that in our country there were so many writers who had no occupation besides literature, who were given special housing or even had dachas, who could go to writers' colonies, had their sanitariums, and so on.

About writers living this way Babel once said, "In the old days, a writer used to live on a crooked little street, next door to a simple cobbler. Across the street might live an obese laundress who, in a man's voice, would scream at her many children out in the yard. While now, what have we got?"

In the summer of 1935 "The Congress for the Defense of Culture and Peace" was held in Paris. A delegation of Soviet writers was to be joined there by Ilya Ehrenburg who was in Paris at the time. When the Soviet delegation arrived, the French writers wanted to know why Babel and Pasternak were not among them. A request that they be added to the delegation was sent off to Moscow. Stalin then ordered that Babel and Pasternak be sent to Paris. Applying for and finally obtaining a passport usually dragged on for months, but now it was done within two hours. While waiting for the passport, Babel and I sat in the little square facing the Ministry of Foreign Affairs by the Kuznetsky Bridge.

When he got back from Paris, Babel told me how Pasternak had almost driven him crazy with his complaining the whole way there: "I am sick, I did not want to make this trip, I don't believe questions of peace and culture can be decided at congresses...I don't want to be there, I'm sick, I can't do it!" In

Germany Pasternak told some correspondents, "Only God can save Russia."

"He just about did me in," Babel said. "Then, when we got to Paris, the three of us — Ehrenburg, Pasternak, and I — met in a cafe to put something together for Boris Leonidovich to use as a speech, since he had fallen apart and just kept repeating: 'I'm sick, I didn't want to come here.' Ehrenburg and I wrote something for him and persuaded him to appear on stage."

"The hall was packed, the upper rows of the balcony full of young students. Vsevolod Ivanov* gave the official speech that had been prepared in Moscow, basically about how well Soviet writers lived — how much money they made, what kind of apartments they had, their dachas, and so on. This speech was exactly the wrong thing to say and made a very bad impression on the French. I felt sorry for poor Ivanov... But when Pasternak came on stage looking at everyone in a confused and child-like way and said, 'Poetry... People search for it every-where... And they find it in the grass...' there was such a burst of applause, such a storm of delight, such shouting, that I knew then and there — that's it, everything's fine, he doesn't have to say another word."

Babel said nothing about his own speech, but I was to learn long afterward from Ilya Ehrenburg that Babel had delivered an extremely witty speech in flawless French that was wildly applauded and cheered, especially by the young.

Babel wrote to his mother and sister from Paris on June 27: "The Congress ended yesterday. My speech, or rather my improvisation (and what's more, improvisation given under the worst possible conditions, at about one in the morning), was a success with the French. I've been allotted a little bit of time to

---

* Viachaslavovich Vsovolod Ivanov (1895–1963), Russian-Soviet writer who headed the Soviet delegation to the Paris cultural Congress.

stay in Paris, and I intend to prowl around like a wolf in search of material — I want to organize my knowledge of *la ville lumière* and maybe write it up and publish it."*

Years later, when Ehrenburg was on his way to France, I asked him if he could find out whether a shorthand transcript of Babel's Congress speech had been preserved. He asked Malraux about it, since he had been one of the organizers, but it turned out that all such materials were lost during the Nazi occupation of Paris.

In April 1936, in the company of André Malraux, Malraux's brother Rolland, and Mikhail Koltsov, Babel traveled to Tesseli to see Maxim Gorky. When he returned, he told me that Malraux had gone in order to propose to Gorky the creation of an *Encyclopedia of the Twentieth Century*, which he felt could be as significant to humanity's spiritual development as Diderot's *Encyclopédie ou dictionnaire raisonné ses sciences, des arts et des métiers* had been in the eighteenth century. As Malraux saw it, such an encyclopedia would become a prime literary, historical, and philosophical weapon in humanism's struggle against fascism. It was assumed that writers and scholars from nearly every country would take part in compiling this monumental work, and that the encyclopedia would be published simultaneously in four languages: Russian, French, English, and Spanish. According to Babel, Gorky approved of the idea and suggested that the Soviet chief editor be Nikolai Bukharin.† Malraux replied that he knew of no other individual with such a broad range of vision.

But it was only in their agreement that the encyclopedia should be created that Gorky and Malraux shared any real mutual understanding. All the questions that Malraux raised in

---

* Babel did publish a piece entitled "*Gorod-svetoch*" which appeared in the journal *Pioneer*, (1937, No. 3).

† Nikolai Ivanivich Bukharin (1888–1938), Soviet statesman and Party leader, editor of *Pravda* and *Izvestiya*, executed under Stalin.

Babel with his sister, Mariya, 1928.

discussion with Gorky — ranging from the freedom of art and the rights of the individual, down to their judgments of the works of such writers as Dostoevsky or Joyce — showed the two to be just about diametrically opposed in their opinions.

During these discussions Koltsov and Babel translated for Malraux. Babel complained to me afterwards that this had been a difficult mission, since one had to be both a translator and a diplomat at the same time. "These talks were not easy for Gorky," Babel said, "while Malraux left Tesseli looking dismal. Gorky's answers did not satisfy him."

During this second visit to the Soviet Union, André Malraux spent a good deal of time with us at our home. Babel loved to fool around with him; he would call him by Russian nicknames such as Andriushka or Andriukha, and he would push a dish of food over to him and start wheedling: "Come on, Andriushka, dig in!" Not understanding Russian, Malraux would only smile and go on with what he was saying. Like all nervous and high-strung people, he talked fast and over-excitedly. Everything interested him: what people thought of Pasternak's poetry, how critics were responding to Shostakovich's music, what was being said at meetings called for writers to consider questions of formalism and realism.

Once when Malraux was visiting, I remember asking him a banal question: how did he like Moscow? The first subway line had just been opened, and it seemed that every foreign visitor was required to go see it, which explained Malraux's curt reply to my question: "A little too much subway." (*Un peu trop de métro.*)

In times to come, Babel was to tell me how, during the Spanish Civil War, Malraux took command of a squadron of airplanes in the International Brigade, and how, in addition, he had flown to New York to speak before American audiences, where the force of his impassioned speeches helped raise a million dollars to aid those fighting for a republic in Spain.

In the summer of 1935 Babel left to travel around the Kiev area to gather materials for a magazine called *The USSR Under Construction*. A special issue on beets was being prepared. It just so happened that I had this time free for a vacation.

In Kiev we stayed at the Hotel Continental. There Babel met with P. P. Postyshev* who assigned him two cars and had some people take him around. Babel told me that Postyshev was very popular in Ukraine, and that he was a good man who liked children and was doing many fine and admirable things for them.

We went off to see the collective farms that were growing beets. The key person in our group was the Moscow photographer, G. Petrusov, since *The USSR Under Construction* consisted mainly of captioned photos. It was Babel's job to help with the general composition of the issue and to "write" the captions.

We stayed overnight on the farms. Babel and Petrusov, together with representatives from Ukraine's Central Committee, would go see the *kolkhoz* administration and engage in detailed discussions about what should be photographed, and where.

On one occasion we were taken to a *kolkhoz* that was so rich it had its own rest home situated in a pine forest. Rows of pine trees were planted in white sand that slowed your feet as you walked through it. Babel told me that the farm did not have much rich land, so its chairman had come up with the idea of cultivating only vegetable and grain seed. Now the *kolkhoz* furnished seed for the whole region and, in return, received bread and everything else it required. We stayed overnight in the empty rest home — empty because, in the summertime (which

---

* Pavel Petrovich Postyshev (1899–1939), from 1933 to 1937 served as Secretary of the Central Committee of the Communist Party of the Ukraine, executed under Stalin.

was now past), it was used as a children's camp, while in the winter, once the harvest was in, only grown-ups came there to rest.

In the morning we went to the *kolkhoz* cafeteria for breakfast. The village consisted of white huts that sunk down amidst a sea of green gardens surrounded by wattle fences. Next to every home there was a wide bench. On the way to breakfast we met a woman all decked out in clean, Ukrainian national garb. She was rushing home to feed her baby. Since we were heading in the same direction, Babel talked to her briefly, and she said that working in a *kolkhoz* was much easier and more enjoyable than running one's own farmstead.

The cafeteria was located in the middle of the *kolkhoz* yard, which was swarming with geese, ducks, and chickens. For breakfast we had a thick soup laden with goose and potatoes, then roast goose, also with potatoes, and watermelon for desert. They fed us the same thing for lunch and dinner, so the next day we couldn't even bear to look at a live goose.

The next morning Babel took along some loose tea and the tea ball that he always traveled with, and we headed off to the kitchen. After some negotiations with the cook we finally managed to get some strong tea. We drank it up greedily.

We stayed for three days at this *kolkhoz*. Babel studied its operations, which, in this case, had nothing to do with beets. During our stay we also attended a celebration to commemorate the opening of a school that went from first grade through high school. The festivities took place in a hall on the second floor of the school. There was a long table covered with refreshments. All the teachers were present, as well as guests from Kiev. Speeches were given in which much was made of the young teaching staff who had studied in Kiev or Moscow and then returned to the village. They were asked to stand and be recognized, which they did with some embarrassment.

We left this *kolkhoz* the following morning and drove out to the fields during the harvesting of the beets. These were piled high all around us. The beets were gathered and stripped by hand. Women with sharp knives skillfully cut off the roots and leaves.

The road back to Kiev lay through a magnificently rich forest. We stayed overnight at a former landowner's estate on the beautiful river Ros, which flowed over boulders. The estate had been turned into a vacation home for railway workers, and we were shown through the manor, the park, and the lilac hill. The latter, densely planted with lilacs, had pathways running through it and benches placed along them.

Back in Kiev, Babel met with old friends from his days in the First Cavalry — Shmidt, Turovsky, and Yakir,* who had invited Babel to the military maneuvers that had been planned for September. These went on for several days. Babel was tired when he returned from them, but he said that he found them "interesting and impressive." He was especially impressed by the tank maneuvers, as well as by the parachute exercises during which a huge number of parachutists had jumped. I recall Babel telling me how, during the maneuvers a certain division commander, Zyuk, had done something wrong. Yakir called for Zyuk and reprimanded him. Zyuk was offended.

"'Comrade General, find yourself another division commander for 300 rubles a month,' he said, and with that, he saluted and left.

"Yakir and Zyuk, a man of high spirits who was liked by everyone, had been the best of friends.

"After the maneuvers we were invited by Dmitri Arkadevich Shmidt, Commander of the Tank Division, to his

---

* All three would later be executed.

encampment on the Dnepr. They fed us soldiers' millet porridge, which smelled of campfire smoke. We ate from army mess-tins, and we drank our tea from tin cups."

Back in Kiev, as we were walking along Shevchenko Boulevard, Babel showed me the building where the Makotinsky family had had an apartment. He had taken refuge there in 1929 and 1930.

Of Mikhail Yakovlevich Makotinsky, a Bolshevik, Babel told the following story: "When the Whites were in Odessa, they put up posters offering 50,000 in gold rubles for the head of Makotinsky. In order to avoid prison, Makotinsky feigned mental illness and managed to outwit the committee of medical experts at the Odessa Psychiatric Hospital. He's a remarkable man; not a man, but an epic poem. Finding himself in the ranks of the Party, Makotinsky gave his energy to a program of 'workers' opposition' for which he was to suffer no small consequences later. When they removed him from his position, he got a job as a janitor on the same street where the hospital was located. When his former colleagues went to work, they would meet him, their former chief, sweeping the street in his janitor's apron."

Makotinsky was arrested in November 1932, while Babel was abroad, and the two were never to meet again. After the arrest of Makotinsky's daughter in 1938, his wife, Ester Grigorevna moved in with us. Of his invitation to her, Babel said, "I'll breathe more easily if she lives with us."

After Kiev, Babel and I headed to Odessa. We checked our luggage at the station while we went to Arkadiya in search of a place to stay. We rented two rooms situated on different levels, each with its own entryway. This section of town was vast and barren. There were no trees or shrubs, and a wooden fence ran along the overhang to the sea whose beach could be reached by way of a long narrow ladder. Our landlady, whose husband was a fisherman, fed us breakfast, but for lunch we went into town where we usually ate in hotels, either the London or the Red.

That summer there were a number of films being shot in Odessa. Many actors and a few directors were staying at the Red Hotel. The Odessa born writer, Yuri Karlovich Olesha, was staying at the London in a narrow room right next to the main entrance on the bottom floor.

After breakfast Babel would work — either by pacing back and forth in his room or by walking for quite some distance along the sea. Once I asked him what he was thinking about all the time. "I want to tell about all this," he said with a sweeping gesture, "and use the minimum number of words, but nothing seems to work. Sometimes I think up whole stories in my mind... "

On the table in Babel's room were papers he had arranged in some particular order, and, from time to time, he would write something down on them. But he had been so stern in forbidding me to look through them, I didn't even glance their way in passing.

Sometimes Babel would go out to sea with our fisherman host to catch chub. This would happen early in the morning before I was awake, and when he returned, he would get me up for a breakfast of fish fried in vegetable oil. When the heat had subsided for the day, we would head into town for lunch. Back in those days Odessa still offered splendid local specialties that Babel so loved — eggplant caviar on ice, eggplant à la grecque, stuffed tomatoes and green peppers.

After lunch the two of us would go for a walk, or sometimes we would walk around in a large group, and, other times we would go get Olesha and head for the Primorsky Boulevard.

There were times when we would head off to distant reaches of Odessa, so Babel could show me his old haunts or the places where his friends and relatives had lived.

We were in Odessa in 1935 when Babel took me to a studio to see the film that V. Vilner had made of Babel's screenplay, "Benia Krik." Babel did not think the film had turned out well.

Babel loved Odessa and, in time, he wanted to settle there. He and the writer L. I. Slavin bought plots of land in Odessa, somewhere behind Station 16. In the fall of 1935 city water services had reached Babel's plot, but he never built a house there. The land itself, which was high up on a steep embankment overlooking the sea, had no vegetation. A path led down to the sea through clay soil, and between the sea and steppe the air had a smell all its own.

※

BABEL OFTEN SAW GORKY, both when he had lived at Molodenovo and, later on, when he had to travel there from Moscow. But Babel made a point of leaving Gorky's house unnoticed whenever there was lots of company or when the "higher-ups" would appear. Once, because of this, he returned to Moscow extremely early. I was home, and when I opened the door, there stood Babel with two pots of flowering cineraria.

"I didn't bring meat. I bought flowers," he announced.

Sometimes, after returning from a visit with Gorky, Babel would tell me what Gorky had recollected about the past during dinner or tea.

The old prerevolutionary ways of Nizhni Novgorod usually dominated Gorky's recollections, which were inexhaustible. On one occasion Gorky might tell how some merchant offered a beautiful governess 100,000 rubles to strip completely naked for him ("And damned if the little minx didn't," Gorky shouted). On another occasion Gorky spoke of a midwife with the name of "Notnow." "That was the name on her sign — 'Notnow.' So, of course, there were times when it was just not now, and that's all there was to it," Gorky laughed. He also reminisced about a village where the only occupation of the inhabitants was to make Cossack whips. Gorky remembered a seditious song he had heard in that village. He recited it placing special stress on the vowel "o."

Out on our new road
Stands a table of old oak,
Stands a table of old oak,
Where thar' writes this new bloke.
He'd write off half the town
To serve the tsar's crown
For the ways of the tsar's crown
Merit nothing but renown...

For Gorky to tell his stories, he had to be in a good mood, and he only told them to a limited group of close friends or to people he found especially congenial.

Another time Babel came home very upset after visiting Gorky's house. This is what he said, "As we were having supper Yagoda* came in and sat down at the table. After taking a good look at what wine we were having, he declared: 'Why are you drinking this Russian swill? Let them bring us French wine, now!' I looked up at Gorky who just sat there drumming his fingers on the table, but he did not say anything."

---

* Genrikh Grigorievich Yagoda (1891–1938), head of the Soviet secret police.

In the spring of 1934, without warning, Gorky's son Maksim became sick and died. On May 18, Babel, who had just recently buried his friend, Eduard Bagritsky,* wrote to his mother about his latest loss: "My main outings have been to the cemetery or to the crematorium. Yesterday, Maksim Peshkov was buried. His death was simply incredible. He wasn't feeling too well, but still, he went for a swim in the Moscow river and this resulted in severe pneumonia. At the cemetery, the old man hardly moved. It was heartrending to see. In Italy Maksim and I had become good friends, we drove thousands of kilometers together, and spent many an evening over a bottle of Chianti..."

Sometimes Babel stayed several days out in Gorki, at Aleksei Maksimovich's home. This would happen when Babel was working on something for Gorky. At these times the two confided most in one another, and their talk tended to focus on literature. I recall one of Gorky's confessions as related to me by Babel, "Today, the old man really opened up to me and said, 'This old fool wrote one really worthwhile thing — "A Story of Unrequited Love" *(Rasskaz o bezotvetnoi liubvi'),* but nobody even noticed.'"

On June 18, 1934 Babel wrote to relatives about this period, "I'm back living at Aleksei Maksimovich's. As they say in Odessa, 'A 1001 nights.' I'll have enough memories to last a lifetime. I am still looking for an out-of-the-way place near Moscow. I've got my eye on something, and I expect to make a decision during the next week. At Aleksei Maksimovich's request I'm spending all my time editing, so I have put the scenario aside."

Babel was referring here to a scenario he had started that was based on Bagritsky's narrative poem, *The Lay of Opanas.*

---

* Eduard Georgievich Bagritsky (Oziubin) (1895–1934), Odessa-born poet.

Once, when Babel returned from Gorky's he related the following incident:

"By chance I had lagged behind and suddenly found myself alone with Yagoda. In order to break an uncomfortable silence I asked him: 'Genrikh Grigorevich, tell me, how should someone act if he falls into your men's paws?' He quickly replied: 'Deny everything, whatever the charges, just say *no* and keep on saying *no*. If one denies everything, we are powerless.'" Later on during the mass arrests under Ezhov,* Babel remembered Yagoda's words and said, "Surely, when Yagoda was in charge, things were still comparatively humane."

Gorky spent the winter and spring of 1936 at his Crimean dacha in Tesseli. Upon his return, Gorky came down with the flu, which quickly became pneumonia. The situation became critical.

On June 17th Babel wrote his mother, "Gorky remains in poor health, but he's fighting like a lion. We are always going from despair to hope. Over the past few days, the doctors have been giving us more cause to be hopeful. Today André Gide is flying in. I'll be going to meet him."

During those days, Babel, like many of Gorky's friends, experienced anguish and alarm; he would often call the hospital in the hope of receiving some comforting news. His hope was in vain, though — the end for Gorky came on June 18.

The following day Babel wrote his mother, "The whole country is in deep mourning, and I more than anyone. This man was my conscience and my judge, a true example for me. I was linked to him by twenty years of unclouded love and friendship. The best way to honor his memory is to live and work. And do both well. Gorky's body is laid out in the Hall of Columns, where huge crowds are filing past his coffin."

---

* Nikolai Ivanovich Ezhov (1895–1940), replaced Yagoda as head of the secret police in 1938. Both were executed.

More than once I have had to listen to people say that Babel used to meet Stalin at Gorky's home, or that the two of them would go visit Stalin in the Kremlin. Babel never said anything to me about this. But to invent a conversation with Stalin and to relate it in an amusing way to some gullible person — that Babel could do. Apparently, that must be the origin of the legend that Stalin talked with Babel and even proposed that Babel write a novel about him — to which Babel is supposed to have said: "I'll think about it, Iosif Vissarionovich." In another story, Gorky had Babel talk about France in Stalin's presence just after his return from there, and while Babel spoke with wit and joviality, Stalin is said to have sat there stony-faced, occasionally uttering something totally irrelevant.

❀

SHTAINER, THE BACHELOR with whom Babel shared the Moscow apartment, was known for his particular punctiliousness, so he was often the object of Babel's jokes and inventions. One example was his response to my asking why Shtainer was not married.

"In his youth he was deeply in love with a girl," Babel told me. "The girl's parents were so strict that they never allowed her to be alone with young Shtainer. Still, after they had known each other for a year or two, the young couple did wind up alone once. But just imagine, when Shtainer got her clothes off it turned out that she had one normal breast and one that was underdeveloped. German pedant that he is, Shtainer could not bear such asymmetry, so he ran away and never saw that girl again. However, since he was in love with her he could not marry anyone else either."

Shtainer's pedantry, his ability to keep house and repair things — all this provided grist for Babel's funny stories. Babel didn't spare me either. When he learned that my father had been orphaned early in life and brought up by a priest from the age of 13 to 17, Babel immediately made my father into a priest. And so Babel told everyone that he had married a priest's daughter, that the priest comes for visits and that they drink tea together from a samovar. For the longest time, Paustovsky believed all this, but my father had died in 1923, long before Babel and I had ever met, and what was more, my father had nothing to do with the church. This didn't matter to Babel, though. He liked the setup — a Jew and a priest.

When he introduced me to someone, he used to say, "I'd like you to meet the girl I want to marry, but she won't have me" — even though I had been his wife for many years.

Babel often said that he was the "merriest of all RABIS* members." He ascribed great importance to merriment. When he sent someone greetings for the new year, he might well write: "I wish you merriment, as much merriment as possible, for there is nothing on earth more important."

Our life together in Moscow was going smoothly. I would leave for work early while Babel was still sleeping. When he got up, he would drink strong tea that he himself concocted with his own special wizardry. Ours was a house of the tea cult. Babel rarely gave away the "premier cru" (as the first cup of freshly brewed tea was called). I did not even figure in the equation here, for I did not care much for tea, which I only later came to appreciate. But if we had an especially important guest, Babel might give him the first cup, saying, "Please note, I'm giving you the 'premier cru.'"

---

* The trade union for workers in the arts.

Babel would eat breakfast at noon and have lunch between five and six. For breakfast or lunch he often invited guests he wanted to see. I only got to meet these people if they came on my days off. I usually came home from work quite late, for I tended to stay till eight or nine at the Metroproject where I was then employed.

In the evening I often called home from work to find out if everything was all right, especially once our daughter was born. "Well, how are things at home?" I would ask, to which Babel might say something like, "Everything's fine, except the baby only ate once."

"How can that be!"

"Once. From morning till night!"

Or, he might say of Shura, our maid, "Things are normal here. Shura and her girlfriend are out in the kitchen playing soccer. They're passing their breasts back and forth to each other."

Sometimes, Babel would call me at work and say to the person answering the phone that it was the Kremlin.

"Antonina Nikolaevna, you have a call from the Kremlin," I would be told in a near whisper. The whole room would grow tense. To me Babel would ask with amusement, "So, everyone get scared?"

Babel was not one to say, "Don't go out," or, "Stay home today." Instead, he would put it another way. "Were you planning to go out this evening?"

"Yes."

"Too bad," he said once. "You see, I've noticed that only good people like you, so you're my litmus test. It's very important for me to find out if Samuil Yakovlevich Marshak* is a good person. He's coming over tonight, and I thought I might introduce you."

---

* Samuil Yakovlevich Marshak (1887–1964), Russian-Soviet writer.

Babel and his son, Misha, 1927.

This was pure trickery on Babel's part, but I, of course, stayed home. I remember that Marshak never came that evening, so Babel was unable to find out if he was a good man.

Sometimes, he would say, "Too bad you're leaving. I was thinking we might have a full-scale tea."

For Babel a "full-scale tea" meant tea served with many different kinds of sweets, especially oriental ones. That was an invitation I never could resist. Babel brewed the tea himself and then we would sit down at the table.

"Real tea-drinking is a lost art," Babel once said. "In times past, it was drunk from the samovar, and without a towel no one would come to the table. The towel was for wiping the sweat off. By the end of the first samovar, they'd be wiping the sweat off their foreheads. By the time the second one arrived, they'd be taking off their shirts. At first, they'd wipe the sweat from their necks and their chests; but when sweat broke out on the stomach, then it was considered that a person had really drunk some tea. That was how they put it: 'Drink tea until it beads on the belly.'"

Babel drank his tea with slices of Antonov apples; he also liked it with raisins.

※

BABEL WOULD OFTEN GO to watch public trials and would sit through various cases and study the judicial setup. In the summer of 1934 he somehow managed to attend the women's judicial consultations at the Solyanka, where E.M. Speranskaya worked as a consultant. She told me that Babel would come and take a seat in the corner, where for hours at a time he would listen to women complain about their neighbors or their husbands.

I can roughly remember the plot of one of Babel's lost stories drawn for his courtroom chronicles. He read me a short tale about a Jewish speculator. The chief judge and his assistants were workers who had had no legal education or courtroom training, while the Jewish plaintiff was extremely eloquent. In this story, the Jew made such an impassioned and hypnotic speech in defense of Soviet power and the evils of speculation that the spellbound judges' panel acquitted him.

＊

ONCE, SOME JOURNALISTS Babel knew arrived back in the USSR from Stockholm with a young Swede named Skugler Tidström. Skugler was so white-haired that he could hardly be called blond. He was tall and his complexion was pinkish. The journalists told Babel that Skugler had come to the Soviet Union as a tourist, but, because he held communist beliefs, he wanted to stay. For some reason Babel let Skugler stay with us and he expected me to look after him.

For days on end this young man would sit in his room and read, occasionally writing things into thick oilcloth-covered notebooks. Once, when I asked him what he was writing, it turned out that he was making an abstract of Lenin's works in Russian. He had studied Russian back in Stockholm, and he was learning to speak it in the Soviet Union.

Babel told me that Skugler came from a wealthy family and that his older brother was a successful manufacturer. Skugler, though, had become a Marxist enthusiast who had turned down a large inheritance. He hated his brother, the exploiter, so he had come here to study the works of Lenin, and he wanted to live and work in the USSR.

"I really don't know what to do with him," Babel said.

By turning to influential friends for help, Babel had managed to extend Skugler's visa several times.

Before long, Skugler met a young woman, a very unattractive one, who had a black cowlick and a pockmarked face. Skugler fell in love. Babel and I saw them together at the racetrack. When this woman cheated on Skugler, he went crazy, so violently crazy that he had to be placed in a psychiatric ward. Babel hired a woman to prepare Skugler's food and bring it to him in the hospital. Babel himself often went to visit him. Once, after returning from the hospital, Babel told me, "The doctors say that Skugler cannot be cured. We'll have to summon his brother."

Skugler's brother arrived with a hospital orderly, who was so well dressed we mistook him for the manufacturer-brother. We had to remove Skugler from the hospital, take him to the train station, and get him into an international railway car. Getting him from the automobile onto the train was dangerous. Babel asked me to accompany Skugler for that part of his journey. The orderly was to wait in the Pullman car while, in a nearby compartment, Skugler's brother was to wait for the right time to appear.

I was terribly anxious. Leading a violently disturbed man by the arm is no laughing matter.

Skugler got out of the car and was glad to see me. As I took him by the arm, he was jovial and began to ask me about my work. And so, chatting away, we gradually made it to the Pullman car, and Skugler entered his compartment.

Babel came in and we said our good-byes and asked him to write. Everything went fine, but later Babel learned what happened after we left. When the train pulled out, the brother entered Skugler's compartment and Skugler attacked him. The struggle was so violent that they broke a window. Skugler had to be kept tied up all the way to Stockholm, where he was placed in a mental institution.

About a month later, Babel started getting letters from Skugler, who told him about his life in the hospital, its routine, the movies he had seen, and so on. He always signed these letters "Skugler dear," probably because when Skugler had stayed with us, during dinner Babel would often say, "Skugler dear *(golubchik Skugler)*, please pass the salt," or words to that effect.

A few months later, Skugler was declared cured and sent home. He immediately signed up with an international brigade to fight in Spain. About a month afterwards, Babel showed up with a letter and a newspaper clipping.

"Skugler alone, with the help of hand grenades, had cleared the path for the rest to escape, but he himself perished. That's how it's written up in this Spanish newspaper."

❋

VENYAMIN NAUMOVICH RYSKIND, a merry raconteur and favorite of Babel's, first came to see him in the summer of 1935 and brought his story, "The Regiment," which he had written in Yiddish. Babel would later translate it into Russian, and the actor, O. N. Abdulov read it both on stage and over the radio.

After Ryskind's first visit, Babel said, "I want to call your close attention to this young man who is Jewish by appearance. He is a very talented writer, and I believe he will amount to something."

Ryskind would come to Moscow, then disappear for a time. Whenever he came to Moscow, he inevitably showed up at our apartment, and Babel was always glad to see him.

Ryskind wrote a play about a child violinist who lived in Poland not far from the Soviet border. Through his friendship with a Polish border guard the youngster hears Soviet songs and plays them for his schoolmates. When the Polish police learn of this, the child is killed. The play was first called *Berchik*, then changed to *A Border Incident*. Theaters in Kharkov and Odessa began to stage the play, but when the war broke out they had to cancel its production.

Besides writing plays and stories, Ryskind also sang, and, sometimes, he would compose music. The subject matter of his stories and songs was always very touching, with a tinge of sorrow. Consequently, his works were not acceptable to the editors of our journals since everything published had to be optimistic and enthusiastic.

Ryskind had also begun work on many screenplays, but he was unable to complete them.

Once Ryskind came up with a rather original way of congratulating me. I had just won a government award, as had many writers that year. It seemed like every writer of any note received a prize — except for Babel, Olesha, and Pasternak. On the day when I read about my award in the newspaper, the door to my room opened and a hand holding a ring of salami appeared, then Ryskind.

"To the prize-winning wife of a prizeless husband," he declared as he handed me the salami.

The three of us immediately prepared tea with the salami, which was the best I could remember having since childhood. It turned out that the salami was the work of Ryskind's brother who was a sausage-maker by trade.

Ryskind played all sorts of tricks.

Laughing, Babel told me how Ryskind had visited the Jewish Theater one winter day and found the actors rehearsing in their winter coats, complaining of the cold. He immediately telephoned the local housing authority and, posing as a representative of the meteorological station, told them in an official voice: "A cyclone is due to hit Moscow, and we are to expect a dramatic decrease in temperature. Under the circumstances, it is vital to keep the heat up in all public institutions, but especially in the theaters." The next day the theater's furnace was blazing.

During his trips to Moscow, Ryskind would stay in a hotel, and it could be very funny to hear him describe how his friends used his hotel room.

Ryskind lived a disorderly life and Babel would encourage him to settle down and make an effort to work every day. One time Babel said to him, "Veniamin Naumovich, I suspect you of leading a dissolute life in Moscow when in fact you should be working. I gave a personal guarantee to a certain editor that you would submit your story on time. For this reason, I will be staying with you in your hotel room to make sure that you are sleeping at night."

Sometime later Ryskind told me, "Isaac Emmanuilovich did indeed come and we got to bed at midnight on the dot. I have to admit that I was extremely worried that one of my playboy friends would take it into his head to drop by or telephone in the middle of the night. I worried so much I couldn't sleep. Sure enough, around two the telephone rings. Babel woke up and said, 'Here we go.' As for me, I was ready to strangle the friend who was discrediting me in Babel's eyes. I ran to the phone, grabbed the receiver, and heard an unfamiliar woman's voice ask for...Babel. Triumphantly, I turned to Babel: 'Isaac Emmanuilovich, it's for you.' He was very embarrassed, put on his glasses and took the receiver: 'Yes? I can't say where he is, but I can guarantee you that at this moment he's not listening to Beethoven's Ninth.' Then, after hanging up, he said, 'Some wife looking for her husband, a film director I was working with today. Antonina Nikolaevna must have given her your number.'"

Babel took an interest in and felt close to this homeless and possessionless fellow with an active imagination.

Once Ryskind told me about an episode from his life that showed how much he himself valued the play of imagination in others.

When he finally was given an apartment in a new house in Kiev, he decided to give a housewarming party, even though he had no furniture whatsoever. He bought several bottles of vodka, sausage, and a big loaf of bread, and set them out on a newspaper on the floor. Then his friends arrived.

"When the guests came," Ryskind said, "they piled their hats and coats in a corner and sat around the newspaper on the floor. There were so many guests that the watchman decided this housewarming wasn't for the poor fellow who had just moved in with only his suitcase, but rather for the Municipal Party Secretary who had just received an apartment in the same section of the building.

"And then suddenly Buchma, the actor, walks in, and something miraculous happens. He takes off his luxurious fur coat and hangs it on a hanger — there being none, of course, it falls right to the floor. Then he hangs his hat above the hanger, then he turns toward the wall, takes out a comb and, as though he were looking in a mirror, starts to comb his hair. Next, he straightens his tie, then, turning this way and that as though he were standing before a large mirror, he adjusts his suit. Then he pretends to open a door from the vestibule into the living room. Here he begins to study the paintings on my walls, which were bare, of course, now moving in close, then moving back. He

[74]

goes over to the window and looks out at the street, then he makes as though to pull my drapes — really heavy ones on metal rings. He approaches the table, picks up a book and starts leafing through it, then heads for the fireplace where he warms his hands before taking a statuette off the mantel and examining it as though it were a real treasure. And that's how the great actor Buchma was able to create for all those present the illusion of a richly furnished apartment."

❋

BABEL WAS ALSO EXTREMELY FOND of Solomon Mikhailovich Mikhoels, and they were close friends. Of Mikhoels' first wife who had died, Babel said, "He can't forget her; he opens the closet and kisses her dresses."

Nevertheless, a few years later Mikhoels met and married Anastasiya Pavlovna Pototskaya. Babel and I used to go see them at their place on Tverskoi Boulevard near Nikitsky Gates. We would drop by evenings and Mikhoels, who loved to sit by candlelight, would light the candles in his old-fashioned candleholders. The room had an alcove and was furnished with heavy antique furniture. I found it somber.

Sometimes Mikhoels would come to our place and sing Jewish folk songs. Other times he would invite us for crepes (*bliny*) at a little restaurant across the way from his apartment. And on still other occasions, after Gorky's death, we would go with him and Anastasiya Pavlovna to Gorky's home in Gorki to spend a few days during the May or November holidays.

Mikhoels' humorous stories would mix with Babel's witty tales. Mikhoels had a gift for impersonation — he could impersonate anybody. He was not good-looking, but because of his talent one did not notice.

Babel instilled in me a love of Jewish theater,* where Mikhoels was the foremost actor and the artistic director. Babel used to say, "Acting done with passion turns up around here only in two theaters — the Jewish and the Gypsy."

Babel especially liked Mikhoels' performance in *The Voyage of Venyamin III*, and the two of us went to see him several times in *Tevye — the Milkman*. I remember vividly Mikhoels' acting in both of those plays, and I also remember how remarkable he was as King Lear.

Usually along with someone else, Babel often came by for me at the end of the work day at Metroproject. He would read our wall newspaper and then come up with funny commentaries of its text.

Once, he and Mikhoels dropped by when there was an article praising me for something or other. It was entitled: "Keep Up with Pirozhkova." I have no recollection whatsoever of why they were praising me at that time. I finished work, and the three of us headed off to eat dinner. I had no idea Babel and Mikhoels had read the article. But the two of them made a game of doing variations on the phrase "Keep up with Piorzhkova" in every way imaginable. Constantly interrupting each other, with different intonations, they would continually put these words into everything they said.

❋

IN THE SUMMER OF 1936 Babel and I agreed that he would go to Odessa and then to Yalta to work with Sergei Mikhailovich Eisenstein on the film *Bezhin Meadow*. I was supposed to join them during my vacation.

---

* The State Jewish Theatre, founded by Mikhoels in 1925.

Babel had begun working on *Bezhin Meadow* with Eisenstein during the winter of 1935–36. Sergei Mikhailovich would come by in the morning and leave in the late afternoon. They used to work in Babel's room, and once, soon after Eisenstein had left, Babel would not let me enter the room.

"Just a second," he said. "I have to destroy the traces of Sergei Mikhailovich's creative inspirations."

A few minutes later Babel let me in and I could see paper burning in the fireplace, while on the table I saw newspapers that had had their edges torn off.

"What does all this mean?" I asked.

"Well, you see, when Sergei Mikhailovich is working, he's always drawing these fantastical and not very decent sketches. They're so good, so gifted, that it's a shame to destroy them, but their content, alas, is salacious, and not for your eyes, so I have to burn them."

That was how I learned not to go into Babel's room right after Eisenstein had left.

It was a cold, rainy October day when I left Moscow to go south. Babel met me in Sebastopol, and we left for Yalta driving in a convertible along an endlessly winding road. Babel gave me no warning before a view of the sea opened up before us. He wanted to see what impression the suddenly appearing panorama would make on me. I was so ecstatic I could hardly breathe. Satisfied with my reaction, Babel said, "I wanted the impression to be as strong as possible, so I didn't say anything beforehand; I asked the driver not to say anything, either."

"Look down there — you can see Foros and Tesseli where Gorky had his dacha. And this is where the famous porcelain plant used to be located, the one that's known both in Russia and abroad."

The shimmering sea, the sun, the greenery, the white curving ribbon of the road — all this seemed incredible after the cold, rainy fall weather I had just left back in Moscow.

The first day after my arrival, as Babel and I were going to dine in a restaurant, he said to me, "Please don't order anything too expensive. We're eating with Sergei Mikhailovich, and, you see, he's a bit stingy."

This was just another of Babel's inventions. We met Eisenstein at the entrance to the restaurant and walked into the dining room together. We had no sooner appeared than some French tourists jumped up and started declaiming: "Vive Eisenstein! Vive Babel!" They were both embarrassed.

Eisenstein lived alone back then, so he had breakfast either with us or with the cameraman, Eduard Kazimirovich Tissé, and his wife, Marianna Arkadevna. When he had breakfast at our place, Eisenstein might say, "You should just taste the bagels at Marianna Arkadevna's." And so I would get up early and run off to the bakery to get warm bagels for breakfast. Then, another time, he might say: "The Tissés had such beautiful tomatoes yesterday." So I would get up at the crack of dawn and go to the market to buy the very best tomatoes. This went on for awhile until Marianna Arkadevna and I had a talk and learned that Sergei Mikhailovich was playing us off against each other. Wise to his ploy, we stopped competing.

After breakfast Babel and Eisenstein would work on the scenario. Babel was supposed to supply the dialogue, but he also helped in creating scenes. In order not to get in the way, I would go for a walk or sit out on the balcony and read. Often they argued and even quarreled with each other. After one such fairly tempestuous scene I asked Babel what they had been fighting about.

"Sergei Mikhailovich is always going beyond the bounds of reality. I keep having to bring him down to earth," Babel said. He explained that they had come up with a scene in which an old woman, the mother of a *kulak*, sits in her hut with a sunflower in her hands; under instructions from the *kulaks*, she removes the sunflower seeds and replaces them with matches whose sulphur tips protrude, and this flower is thrown beside a fuel tank at a Tractor Station so that one of the *kulaks* can set it on fire with a match or a cigarette butt. The match-filled sunflower bursts into flame, sets fire to the fuel tank and eventually burns down the whole Tractor Station.

"So this old woman is sitting in her hut and replacing the seeds with matches," Babel said, "and she's continually looking over at the icons. She fully understands that what she is doing is utterly un-Christian, and she fears that the Lord will punish her. Here, fantasy gets the better of Eisenstein, and he says: 'Suddenly the ceiling of the hut cracks, the Heavens open, and Almighty God appears in the clouds ... The old woman faints.' That's how Eisenstein wanted to shoot the scene. Meanwhile, he's got little Stepok, wounded, wandering through the wheat field wearing a halo around his head. Sergei Mikhailovich himself has told me many times he prefers what isn't there in actuality — the *isn'tness*. He is so strongly drawn to the fantastic, the unreal. But unrealism around here is unrealistic," concluded Babel.

Bezhin Meadow was shot on days when the weather was good. They had chosen a site for a building to house the agricultural machinery and next to it tar-covered barrels of fuel had been set out. The area was strewn with straw and, scraps of metal were lying about. On top of the Tractor Station was a dovecote. Using a megaphone, Eisenstein presided over the shooting from his director's platform. Sometimes, Babel and I would come and watch. I also recall Eisenstein using a number of local walk-ons for crowd scenes.

In the evening we would go to a projection room to view the material that had just been shot. It was exceptionally good. White doves flying up, white horses racing about madly, and the white shirt of the actor Arzhanov — all that on the background of the black smoke curling from the burning Tractor Station. It was Eisenstein's idea to exploit black and white contrasts to convey an opposition between what was bright and happy, and what was dark and sinister. To this end, he was constantly on the lookout for white accessories — horses, goats, doves...

After we had seen the results of the actual shoot, Babel said to me, "While we were filming, there was no way one could have reckoned on the final results being so magnificent. That's master craftsmanship for you!"

In the spring of 1935, before Babel, Eisenstein and I had gone to Yalta, the three of us attended a performance of the Chinese theater company headed by Mei Lanfang. During the intermission, when Sergei Mikhailovich decided to go backstage, Babel said to him:

"Take Antonina Nikolaevna with you, she'll find it interesting." And so the two of us went backstage together.

We found the actors in small dressing rooms, and all of them had their doors open. They were barefoot and wore long robes, some of them of an everyday sort, others meant for the stage. Some of the performers were sitting, others were walking about. Sergei Mikhailovich greeted them all, and I followed suit. Sergei Mikhailovich began talking to Mei Lanfang himself. They talked for a long time, and, as I understood it, they spoke in Chinese. All the while, Mei Lanfang was smiling and bowing.

Babel with his daughter, Natasha, 1932.

I was overwhelmed. I had known that Eisenstein could speak just about any European language, but Chinese? I said to Babel, "Sergei Mikhailovich was speaking Chinese to Mei Lanfang, and he was good at it, too."

"His Japanese is just as good," Babel responded with a laugh.

I would later learn that Eisenstein was really speaking to Mei Lanfang in English, but was speaking with a Chinese intonation, which could easily mislead someone who didn't know any better. Babel, of course, was well aware of Eisenstein's ability to mimic the intonation of one language while actually speaking another.

Once Babel and I visited Eisenstein at his home in Potylikha. A maid let us in, and when we went through the corridor and dining room and knocked at the door of his study, Sergei Mikhailovich asked, "Babel, are you alone or with Antonina Nikolaevna?" When he found out that I was with Babel, he said, "Wait just a minute, please," and after a few minutes he let us in.

The room was a large one with a big writing table; the walls were hung with paintings and photographs, and suddenly I noticed that a number of these were turned towards the wall. So that was what Sergei Mikhailovich had been doing before he had let us in! I was overcome with curiosity, and finding a moment when the two men were busy talking about something, I quickly turned one of the picture frames around. In it was a photograph of a naked man, very fat and hairy, sitting on a chair with his back to the viewer. The spectacle was not a pleasant one, and I turned the photograph back against the wall.

During that visit Sergei Mikhailovich showed us some souvenirs he had brought back from Mexico. They included real fleas in wedding dress. The bride was wearing a white gown, a veil, and fleurs d'orange; the groom was wearing a black suit with a white shirt front and bow tie. This couple was kept in a receptacle that was even smaller than a match box, and you had to use a magnifying glass to view them.

"You have to admit it's no small feat, although it's not the same as shoeing a flea," Babel joked. "Still, I'd have to say that with Leskov's Russian smith we keep the lead."*

That evening Sergei Mikhailovich told us many interesting things about Mexico and also about Charlie Chaplin, whom he knew quite well. He spoke of how Chaplin would never spare himself to make a scene work. For example, if he had to fall or jump into the water, he would do it dozens of times to perfect every movement. "He was just as unsparing of other actors," Eisenstein said.

In his letters to me Babel referred to Sergei Mikhailovich as "Eisen." He had great respect for Eisenstein, whom he thought of as brilliant in every way, while of himself he said that he was a mere mortal who "worshipped at Eisenstein's altar."

Eisenstein felt the same in regard to Babel — he greatly valued Babel's literary prowess, his gift as a storyteller; he was also lavish in his praise of Babel's play, *Sunset* (*Zakat*), whose social significance he equated with that of Zola's novel *L'argent* in that Babel had succeeded in illuminating capitalist relationships through the experience of a single family. Eisenstein was critical of the Moscow Art Theater II for its weak staging of the play, particularly for failing to convey to the audience every single word of its unusually terse text.

---

* A reference to a classic Russian short story by N. S. Leskov (1831–1893).

While we were still in Yalta, there was one day when Babel and I were out walking and we saw a woman who was pushing her crippled husband in a wheelchair. The man's legs were covered by a blanket and his face was pale.

"Look," Babel said, "how touching! Would you be capable of doing the same?"

I remember thinking to myself, "Can he possibly be imagining a similar fate for himself?"

✻

IN NOVEMBER WE WENT by steamship from Yalta to Odessa. On the way there our ship was hit by a storm of near gale force. Babel felt awful the whole voyage. Quite green, he lay in our cabin sucking on a lemon. The storm had no effect on me and so, unfazed, I had my meal in the dining room. When I told Babel that I was the only one eating in the dining room, he remarked, "One of a kind. A true Siberian."

When we got to Odessa we moved into a two-bedroom apartment not far from Gogol Street and the Primorsky Boulevard. We would prepare our own breakfast, but we made private boarding arrangements for our main meals. Babel would work in the mornings while I strolled around Odessa. After lunch and in the evenings we would go walking together.

On Gogol Street there was a bakery where we bought our bread and, just nearby, was a bagel shop where you could buy warm bagels sprinkled with poppy seeds. Babel loved these bagels, and he usually ate them right in the shop or out on the street. One time when we had gone into the bagel shop, a middle-aged man walked in with us and looked around in a perplexed way before asking the saleswoman:

"Citizeness, is bread planning to be here?"

Babel whispered to me, "Now that's Odessa talking."

On another occasion we passed some young men just as one of them took off his suit jacket and said to another, "Zhora, hold my macintosh for me, while I demonstrate my character to this guy." And then a brawl began.

Babel insistently coached me to listen for the language of Odessa. As a result I started to tell him the interesting phrases I picked up, and he would write them down. For example, some school kids were walking through the courtyard when one of them said: "*Okh!* Mama's really going to stew my prunes."

Odessa-speak never failed to amuse Babel.

There were days when we made special excursions to visit with fishermen and some of Odessa's old-timers, Babel's friends from long ago. I recall one elderly vintner and philosopher, a man known far and wide, who had come up with almost two hundred varieties of grapes. We met another fellow who had married the beautiful Anna Tsakni, Ivan Bunin's* first wife, and who was himself a grand-nephew of the city's founding father, Jose De Ribas.

Babel's talks with the fishermen were very technical, touching on catching and smoking various types of fish, as well as on storms and all sorts of other happenings at sea.

While we were in Odessa Babel would recall his childhood. "My grandmother was convinced that I would bring fame and fortune to our family. As a result, she treated me very differently than she did my sister. When my sister would ask, 'Why is it all right for him to do that when I can't?' my grandmother would say to her in Ukrainian: *'Rovnya konya do svinya* — you can't compare a horse with a pig.'"

---

* Ivan Alekseevich Bunin (1870–1953), a Russian writer who left the country in 1920.

One day Babel broke into an uncontrollable fit of laughter, and as he was laughing he explained to me that he had remembered how once he had taken some just-cooked lamb chops to treat his pals out in the yard. When she saw what he was up to, his grandmother ran outside and began chasing after his friends. She managed to catch one of them and began prying the meat right out of his mouth.

For all I knew, this might have been pure invention. By this time I had been around Babel long enough to know that, for the sake of a piquant or funny story, he would never spare friends and relatives — or me either.

Odessa also evoked frequent memories of his mother.

"My mother was a gifted comic," he said. "Whenever she imitated a neighbor or acquaintance, the way they walked or talked, she always got it right. She was more than just good at it, she was talented. Had the times and conditions been different, she could have become an actress."

Babel had two aunts in Odessa, his mother's sisters, but he rarely visited them, and if he did, it was always alone. He didn't visit his second cousin, Ada, very often either. Babel did keep fairly close ties with his Aunt Katya in Moscow, also from his mother's side of the family. Whenever this aunt chanced to visit someone to whom Babel had recklessly given away a piece of furniture, she would say: "You must forgive my nephew. He is really quite mad. This cabinet you have here is a family heirloom. I'll have to ask you to return it to me." And so it was that Aunt Katya managed to repossess some of the family furniture that Babel had given away.

On one occasion while we were in Odessa, Babel was asked to read some of his stories in public. He returned with a whole pile of written questions that had been handed to him after he had read. One of them was unforgettably Odessian: "Comrade Babel, how is it that people are hauling *Quiet Flows the Don* around by the armloads, while all you've given us is 'Benia Krik'?"

On another occasion in Odessa I broke my rule of never discussing Babel's literary work with him and asked: "Are your stories autobiographical?"

"No," Babel said.

From his account, it turned out that even such stories as "The Basement" and "Awakening," which seemed to reflect his childhood, were not actually autobiographical. Perhaps a few details were, but not the whole story plot. When I asked him why he wrote the story in the first person, he replied, "That way the stories come out shorter, you don't have to describe who the narrator is, what he looks like, what kind of background he has, what he's wearing . . . ."

Babel told me that the plot for the story "My First Fee" ("*Moi pervyi gonorar*") had been suggested to him by the journalist P. I. Staritsyn, back in Petrograd. In Staritsyn's version, he had gone to a prostitute, gotten undressed, but then saw himself in the mirror looking like "an overwrought pink swine." Disgusted, he quickly dressed, told the woman he was a male prostitute, and left. Sometime later he was on a tram when he saw this woman at a stop along the way. Their eyes met and she called out to him: "Greetings, little sister." That was it.

❋

ON OBUKHOV STREET, not far from our Moscow apartment, there was a building that had been allotted to political émigrés. People of many different nationalities came from there to visit us. All were communists who had been persecuted in their homelands. Generally, we would sit together in the kitchen downstairs. I would return from work to find a whole flock of these people talking away in their various mother tongues. Babel or Shtainer would brew coffee, they would get food from the refrigerator, and interminable discussions would ensue. On one such occasion, the Chinese poet Emi Siao turned up.

Siao was a short, well-built man with attractive features. He had fled the China of Chiang Kai-Shek for temporary residence in Moscow. He began to visit us regularly. He would recite his verse for us both in translation and in Chinese, the latter especially for Babel who wanted to hear how it sounded in the original.

Emi Siao's Russian was very good, but he was eager to go back to China. The Chinese Communist Party wanted to safeguard him as its poet though, so it prevented him from returning home. Siao dreamed passionately of a communist future for China.

Once, during dinner, Babel asked him, "Tell me, Siao, what constitutes an ideal woman for a Chinese man?"

I found Siao's reply memorable: "A woman must be so elegant and so frail that a zephyr would make her fall over."

In the summer of 1937 Emi Siao went on vacation to the Black Sea. When he returned in the fall he brought with him a plump young woman named Eva whom he introduced to us as his wife. Her blue eyes were set in a beautiful face, and her hair was close-cropped like a boy's. The rest of her was rather heavyset. When they left Babel remarked:

"Ideals are one thing, life is another."

Soon afterwards, Emi Siao invited us for a Chinese dinner that he made himself. This was the first time we had visited the building for the political émigrés. Emi Siao had one room there, a room he now shared with Eva, a German Jewess who had fled to Stockholm to stay with her brother, a well-known musician.

While visiting the USSR as a tourist she had met Emi Siao in the Caucasus, and soon the two were married.

For dinner we had fish soup — *tripang* — garnished with radishes; fish and roast chicken with rice — both the chicken and fish were very finely chopped and had been seasoned with special Chinese spices. We were all given chopsticks, but only Emi Siao knew how to use them. The rest of us retreated to the safety of forks. For desert Eva prepared a European dish: thick cream laced with wine and vanilla on which we sprinkled corn flakes just before eating.

That winter the Writers' Union assigned Emi Siao an apartment in Lavrushinsky Lane. Babel and I were invited to the housewarming, where once again Emi Siao prepared Chinese food. However, this time it was the tea we found particularly impressive. We were all given small round Chinese teacups and then a large teapot with a sealed spout was brought in. When the cork was removed from the spout and the tea was being poured, an inexpressibly wonderful aroma spread around the room. It is really impossible to describe what this strong and remarkable tea was like. We drank it as they do in China — without sugar.

In very late 1938 or very early in 1939, Emi Siao left for China with his family, which now included a son. At first they had to stay in the Communist-controlled part of the country, but eventually they moved to Beijing. Emi Siao and Eva had two more sons. Eva herself became an excellent photographer for a Beijing newspaper, and she was able to return to the USSR for a few short visits.

ONCE WHEN VALENTINE KATAEV'S* two-year-old daughter ran into his room and saw from the window that the first snow had turned everything white, she asked him excitedly, "Papa, does this mean it's my birthday?"

Babel was filled with delight when he heard this. He loved children, yet the way his life turned out, he wasn't able to bring up a single one of his own.

Babel's first marriage was in 1919 to Evgeniya Borisovna Gronfain. Her father was a wealthy Kievan who owned factories that produced farming implements. Babel's father bought them and then sold them in his store in Odessa. It was through this connection, in all likelihood, that the two young people met when Babel was studying at the Commercial Institute in Kiev, where Evgeniya Borisovna, having finished *gymnasium*, was studying painting in a private art school.

When he finished the Commercial Institute in 1916, he went off to Petrograd where he met Maxim Gorky who published Babel's first stories in his journal *Letopis'*. He also worked there in 1918, for Gorky's newspaper, *Novaia zhizn'* and as a translator for the Cheka; it was only after this that he returned to Odessa and married.

In May 1920 Babel went off to serve in the Red Cavalry as a correspondent for its newspaper *Krasnyi kavalerist (The Red Cavalryman)*. For this mission Ugrosta had given him official documents under the assumed name Kirill Vasilevich Liutov.

In 1922 Babel, now accompanied by his wife and sister, went to the Caucasus as a special correspondent for the newspaper *Zarya vostoka*.

---

* Valentine Petrovich Kataev (1897–1986), a Russian-Soviet writer.

When his father fell ill in 1923, Babel was back in Petrograd, and by the time he could return to Odessa at the beginning of 1924, his father was no longer alive.

After his father's death Babel and his family (his wife, his mother, and his sister), moved to Moscow. At first they lived at the home of his friend Isaac Leopoldovich Livshits,* but they soon settled outside of Moscow in a small town called Sergiev Posad (Zagorsk).

In December 1924, Babel's sister Mariya (Mera) left for Brussels to be with her fiancé, Grigori Romanovich Shaposhnikov, and in August 1925 she was joined by Babel's mother. In the same year, his wife, Evgeniya Borisovna, left for Paris. Her excuse for leaving was that she wanted to further her study of painting in Paris, but it seems that there must have been other reasons as well. In any case, it was well known that even before Evgeniya Borisovna's departure for Paris in December 1925, Babel moved from Sergiev Posad to Moscow to live with Tamara Vladimirovna Kashirina. On July 13, 1926, Babel's own birthday, a boy was born to him and Tamara Vladimirovna. The child was given the name of Emmanuel in honor of Babel's own father.

In 1927 Babel went to Kiev to arrange for the funeral of Evgeniya Borisovna's father. Then, having disposed of all the possessions in the family apartment, he had to accompany his wife's sick and elderly mother to Paris so that she could be with her daughter.

Domestic life had failed to work out for Babel and Tamara Vladimirovna, and when he left for Paris he was hoping to patch things up with his first wife. Babel stayed in Paris until

---

* Isaac Leopoldovich Livshits (1892–1979), Babel's close friend since his days at Odessa Commerce College.

the end of 1928. During this time Tamara Vladimirovna married the writer Vsevolod Ivanov who adopted the little boy, gave him his own family name and changed his first name from Emmanuel to Mikhail. In this way, Babel lost his first child whom he was not even permitted to visit.

In Paris, Babel's relationship with Evgeniya Borisovna was smoothed over, but she was, obviously, still not willing to move back to Moscow, so Babel came home alone. In July 1929, Evgeniya Borisovna gave birth to a daughter, Natasha, whom Babel was only able to meet in 1932 when he again went to Paris.

From our earliest acquaintance, Babel never spoke to me about Tamara Vladimirovna or his little boy, but when he was away in Paris in 1932, his closest friends immediately told me everything about them. Respecting his wishes that I not know, I never spoke of them in our conversations.

By contrast, I knew everything about Natasha. Babel would always show me her photographs and repeat everything that Evgeniya Borisovna wrote in her letters about her, and would ask me to buy toys and little books for her.

Natasha was an enchanting child, and I liked her so much that I wanted just the same kind of cheerful and sly little girl myself. In January 1937, our own daughter was born. I wanted to name her Mariya, but Babel said that Jews did not name children after living relatives and his own sister was named Mariya. When I was in the maternity hospital, Babel brought me a book, Sterne's *A Sentimental Journey*, and in it I came across the name Lydia and thought that we should call our child Lida. Babel agreed.

I remember when Babel came to the maternity hospital to take us home. I was already dressed in my street clothes when I suddenly saw the front vestibule door open and Babel come in carrying so many boxes of chocolates that he had to steady the top of the stack with his chin. He immediately began giving them away right and left, to all the doctors and nurses he met on his way — both to those we wanted to thank and those who had nothing to do with us. That was Babel through and through!

The first person to come to our home and congratulate us was Eisenstein. He arrived and put an oddly shaped object all wrapped up in paper and red ribbon on the table. When we unwrapped it, we found a child's white chamber pot — inside of which was a little bouquet of violets. Where had he managed to buy violets in January? And where, for that matter, had he managed to buy so unusual an object as a child's chamber pot? Our Soviet stores did not carry such necessities back then either.

In the summer of 1937, when Lida was five months old, Babel rented a dacha in Belopesotskaya, near Kashira. Belopesotskaya was located along the Oka River. Babel took enormous pleasure in going swimming and in sunbathing on the pure white sand of the river shore.

We would often go for walks in the woods, but before we could get very far, Babel would start getting nervous and say, "We've done it! Now we're lost and we'll never find our way."

Accustomed to wide open spaces, Babel was clearly a bit fearful of the forest, where he never seemed comfortable. It was always with great surprise and even respect that he noticed how, no matter where we went, I could always find our way and always felt at home. "Are you a sorceress?" he would ask. "Do the birds tell you the way?"

There was nothing magical to it. I had just grown up in the Siberian taiga.

ONCE, WHILE WE WERE at our dacha, Babel was leafing through a huge, just published book by one of our better-known writers and said, "If I wrote like this, I could write a thousand pages, too." Then, after a moment, he added, "No, I take it back. I'd die of boredom. The only thing I could write about endlessly is the chatter of a silly woman."

At ten months Lida was walking and as her first birthday approached she was running beautifully. At that age she still didn't talk, but the faces she made caused us great amusement. She apparently understood that she was making the people around her laugh, so she became increasingly resourceful at doing so. This caused Babel to remark, "Now we have it good. When company comes we don't have to entertain them. Just send Lida in and let her do it."

Sometimes, he would say, "When she grows up, I won't let her go. I'll dress her in rags so nobody will want to marry her."

❋

LION FEUCHTWANGER CAME TO MOSCOW and paid Babel a visit. He was not very tall, had bright red hair, and, although he was an extremely fastidious man, he wore a suit that seemed too small on him.

They conversed in German, which Babel spoke freely. I myself had a reading knowledge of German, and was then, at Babel's urging, studying German literature with the help of an instructor. Still, I had great trouble understanding Feuchtwanger; though I knew words individually, I couldn't fit them together. I found this irritating, especially since Babel would often ask

Babel with his daughter, Lida.

me for help in spelling a word when he wrote to someone in German. But I had no practice in conversing, so I just could not keep up.

Babel told Feuchtwanger: "Antonina Nikolaevna is studying German in your honor." Feuchtwanger said he would send me his works when he returned to Germany. And indeed, he did send me several dark-blue volumes that, as I recall, had been published in Hamburg. However, I only managed to read *Success* (*Erfolg*) before Babel passed them on to Sofiya Khristianovna, the wife of the artist Lisitsky. Since she was German, Babel just could not resist. And shortly thereafter, she was given 24 hours to get out of Moscow.

After Feuchtwanger left, I asked Babel to tell me what he had said that was particularly interesting.

"He spoke of his impressions of the USSR, and of Stalin. I heard many bitter truths."

Babel did not elaborate on this statement.

❋

IF WRITERS VISITED the Soviet Union during those years, they always came to see Babel. Once André Gide came to have dinner with us, and I remember a meal of trout with a white sauce and homemade Russian *kvas*. About Gide, Babel said to me: "He's a smart one, that devil! Compared to him, Gorky seems like a village priest."

The writers Leon Mussinac and Oskar Maria Graf also came to visit, the latter wearing his national costume that included a short skirt. The well-known French politician Edouard Herriot came with a present — a big round box of coffee beans. When we had prepared the coffee, which was incredibly fragrant and delicious, Babel said: "Our leaders think

Russians don't know anything about coffee, which explains why the government buys fourth-rate coffee from Brazil. Now you know what real coffee tastes like."

A tremendous variety of people were drawn to Babel, not only because he was a man of high culture and a wonderful storyteller, but also because of his character; his was a delightful nature and his charm worked on absolutely everyone. Babel loved life, believed that people were born for merriment and the pleasures of life. He delighted in funny stories and situations, which he loved to invent. But sometimes his pranks put people in awkward situations.

Once, at a family dinner attended by an elderly aunt, a dentist, and a very serious, proper lady, one of the guests told how, during the Revolution, someone had had to hide in a brothel in order to avoid the police. Suddenly Babel said: "I bet I know which one! My aunt here ran one herself in Odessa . . . " You can imagine how his aunt took it. She was dumbstruck, and her whole face became covered with red blotches.

Once an old school friend from Siberia was visiting me. Babel walked in unexpectedly and sat down on a chair, talked to us for a while, made us laugh, then stood up and began to walk backwards towards the door. We looked at him, puzzled. "Please excuse me, but I can't turn around. I have a huge hole in the seat of my pants!" And that was how he made his exit.

On another occasion in Kiev, in 1938, Babel had been invited to dine at the house of a former schoolmate, Miron Naumovich Berkov. According to Berkov's widow, Klavdiya Yakovlevna, the men went into the bedroom to rest. Later that evening they had tea and then the hosts walked Babel to his hotel. After strolling together and chatting, they were saying good-bye when, as Klavdiya Yakovlevna put it, "I noticed that Babel had a piece of clothing draped over his arm, and I recognized its buttons. I said, 'Babel, that's my dress!' And he replied, 'You see, I know a certain woman who's always insisting I bring her gifts. Since I'm broke, I decided I'd give her this dress.'" Klavdiya Yakovlevna took her dress back, and for some time after she and Babel laughed at his caper.

Babel often permitted himself these kinds of pranks, and the more implausible his ideas appeared, the more amusing he found them.

He could, for example, introduce his mother to someone by saying: "This is my younger sister," or, present his sister as, "Our little miscarriage." He introduced the writer S. G. Hecht to Esenin* as his son, and so on.

Babel loved to try acting out a whole range of roles: a cripple, a miser, a sick man, a jealous lover. If he and I went for a walk around the city, he might suddenly begin limping, and limp in a whole variety of ways, either as if he had one leg shorter than the other, or as if one leg was twisted and had to be dragged. Passersby would looked on in surprise, and while he kept the most serious expression on his face, I would be dying of laughter.

If he tried the role of someone sick, he might begin groaning in all kinds of different tones. I would run to his room in concern, while he would continue groaning in front of me a little while longer. Then he would suddenly burst out laughing and say, "I have just been demonstrating for you 'the Jewish groan.'"

Playing the miser, he would get on a tram and not take a ticket, then suddenly jump off while the tram was moving if the ticket inspector came on board; which is to say that I would have to jump off too. Alleging he was broke, he might ask some lady sitting next to him to buy him a ticket.

---

* Sergei Aleksandrovich Esenin (1895–1925), Russian-Soviet poet.

He could also act superstitious; he kept a horseshoe at home for good luck and might come back to the house if a black cat crossed his path or if one of the domestics asked where he was going.

❋

AT THE START OF 1936 Shtainer left on business for Vienna. For the period that he was to be away, he invited a Hungarian couple named Sinkó who needed a place to stay to move into the apartment. He got Babel's approval and it was decided that the Sinkós should occupy the lower floor.

After we got to know the Sinkós better, Babel told me their story. Ever since the crushing of the Hungarian Commune in 1919, Erwin Sinkó, who was one of its members, had been a political émigré. He had lived as an émigré in France, Austria, and Germany where he had written a novel called *Die Optimisten*, which he was now trying to publish. It was for this purpose that he had come to the Soviet Union, armed with a letter of recommendation from Romain Rolland. He was granted a six-month stay in Russia as the guest of an organization charged with looking after foreign cultural ties. Thanks to Gorky, Sinkó had been given a further six months, but after this extension, Sinkó ran into difficulty when no publisher had agreed to print *Die Optimisten*. His wife, Irma Yakovlevna, an x-ray pathologist, did find a position in a Moscow institute.

Babel had heard somewhere how the Sinkós had come to be married, and he told me the story. During World War I Erwin and Irma had been underground revolutionaries who had planned to publish a journal modeled after the Zimmerwald Programme, calling for the proletariat to pursue peace by turning their weapons against the capitalist exploiters. Irma's dowry money was to be used in support of this cause, but her father was against her marrying a poor student like Erwin. To counter this, one of the members of the movement, an engineer by the name of Gyula Hevesi, agreed to act as Irma's fiancé. At the time Hevesi was already fairly well known as an inventor and director of a research lab specializing in lighting technology. When the pseudo-fiancé was introduced to Irma's father, he was only too happy to encourage such a promising young man as his daughter's suitor. Sometime later, the wedding was held and the young couple went off on their honeymoon. At the nearest station, the pseudo-fiancé got off the train and Erwin Sinkó took his place in the compartment.

Babel thought very highly of Irma Yakovlevna, but he had this to say about Erwin: "He prefers the role of the unappreciated genius to working. He's living off his wife."

Babel found Sinkó's novel boring, but he nevertheless tried to find it a publisher or a producer for a movie adaptation. But nothing came of this.

At the beginning of 1937, the Sinkós left for France, then moved to Yugoslavia where Erwin got a job teaching in the university at Novi Sad.

That same year Shtainer was not allowed to return to the USSR following his business trip to Austria, so Babel and I remained alone at Nikolo-Vorobinsky. We continued to occupy the upper floor, and, in due course, new tenants moved into the two downstairs rooms.

At first, I believed Babel's romantic story about the Sinkós, but then I began to doubt it, and eventually I decided that it was just another in his long string of invented plots. So one can imagine my surprise when I visited Budapest in 1966 and actually met Gyula Hevesi, Irma's pseudo-fiancé. He himself told me the same story about the Sinkós' marriage. So it would seem that

Babel's anecdotes about other people were not always pure make-believe.

Later still, in 1968, a Yugoslavian professor told me that Erwin Sinkó had died from a cerebral hemorrhage while in Zagreb. Irma Yakovlevna fulfilled her husband's last will and testament, namely she gave his rich book collection to the Novi Sad Philosophy Department where Erwin had held a position as professor and department chair, and gave his manuscripts to the Yugoslavian Academy of Sciences in Zagreb, of which Erwin was a member. Using all their savings, she created the Erwin Sinkó Endowment Fund to support outstanding students of Hungarian language and literature. Having taken care of these matters, she took poison and died.

❋

BABEL HAD ALWAYS RESISTED living in a writers' residence, whether it was the one on Lavrushinsky Street or the new one in Peredelkino. It was only because of our daughter that he ended up taking a dacha in Peredelkino. On April 16, 1938 he wrote about this to his mother and sister:

"I'm torn between the desire to go to Odessa and the need to take care of matters that are detaining me here in Moscow. In a few days I'll be moving into a dacha of my own, so to speak. Until now I had not wanted to live in a so-called writers' settlement, but I changed my mind when I found out that the dachas are quite distant from each other and one doesn't have to rub elbows with one's confreres. The settlement, which is about 20 kilometers from Moscow, is called Peredelkino. It is located in a forest where the snow is still hard-packed ... That's our spring for you. The sun has been an infrequent visitor, and it's high time he moved in with us."

We moved into the dacha before it was completely finished. I was in charge of looking after its completion, including some final changes that Babel had requested. He chose the smallest room as his study and he ordered a dovecote that was to stand right next to the dacha.

We did not have a stick of furniture, but very shortly after we moved in, Gorky's wife, Ekaterina Pavlovna, called to say that the Committee for the Red Cross had been shut down and its furniture was for sale. She and I went and picked out two desks. They were simpler than standard writing desks, but still, they each had carved legs and a drawer in the center. Pointing to one of them, Ekaterina Pavlovna said: "I worked at that table for 25 years." We also picked up a black couch with a carved wooden back, a small armchair with a leather seat, and a few other pieces. Satisfied with our purchases, we left and I dropped Ekaterina Pavlovna off at her home on Mashkov Lane (now Chaplygin Street).

It is from this outing that I date my personal acquaintance with Ekaterina Pavlovna.

Babel left the couch and Ekaterina Pavlovna's desk at our place on Nikolo-Vorobinsky. Almost all the furniture in his dacha study was new, and it remained unfinished — just the way he had gotten it from the local cabinetmaker. The study had a low wooden-plank bed with a mattress — a rather firm one, the kind Babel liked; by the window there was a simple working table that ran the whole width of the room; there were low bookcases and the leather-seated chair we had bought from the Red Cross. A fairly small oriental rug from Turkmenistan lay on the floor.

※

IN THE YEAR 1936 MOSCOW SAW the trials of the so-called "enemies of the people," and every night friends and acquaintances of ours were arrested.

Babel was acquainted with many people, among them important politicians, military personnel, journalists, and writers. He used to say to me: "I am not afraid of arrest as long as they let me keep writing." And even before that, after the death of Gorky, he had once said: "Now they are not going to let me live."

It seemed as if the door to our house never closed. Not only did the wives of Babel's comrades come by, but also the wives and parents of prisoners unknown to him. These visitors cried as they begged Babel to intervene on behalf of their loved ones. Babel would get dressed up and, literally bent down by it all, would head off to see some of his former comrades in arms who had, as yet, survived and still held influential positions. Babel would turn to them either for help or for information. He would come back looking extremely grim, but he tried to find words to comfort the people who had turned to him.

Babel was suffering terribly during this ordeal, and I actually used to picture his heart as large, wounded, and bleeding. It was apparent that Babel did not want me to suffer, for he tried to avoid talking about the whole issue. Still, I asked, "Why is it that during the trials they all confess and heap shame on themselves? Really, there's never been anything like this. If they are political opponents, why don't they use the opportunity to tell the whole world about their views and their principles?"

"I myself don't understand it," Babel replied. "They are all intelligent and brave. Perhaps it's that they are influenced by their Party training and by a desire to save the Party overall?"

I knew that he didn't believe the accusations but I also knew that he didn't understand why everybody was confessing to such fantastically crazy accusations. There were many of us then who didn't understand this. In those years none of us could allow even into our minds the possibility of torture in Soviet prisons. In the tsarist period, yes — that was possible; but in the Soviet state? It was simply unthinkable. Hypnotized by this kind of belief, there were even those among us who refused to acknowledge anything that was happening or accept the evidence before them.

When Yakov Livshits, the Director of National Transportation, was arrested, Babel could not contain himself and said, "They expect me to believe that Livshits wanted to restore capitalism to our land! He comes from a working-class family, and believe me, nobody was worse off under tsarism than working-class Jews. And during the Revolution, you had to restrain Yakov from summarily executing the bourgeois every chance he got. That's how much he hated them. And now I'm supposed to believe that he wanted the restoration of capitalism. How monstrous!"

In January of 1939 Ezhov was removed from his position as head of State Security. Babel had long known Ezhov's wife, Evgeniya Solomonovna, and he used to visit their home. Having married Ezhov and become part of the official elite, she then wanted to have her own literary salon. For this reason Babel was invited to Ezhov's home on days when they were having company. Ezhov himself rarely took part in these gatherings, most often arriving toward the end.

Mikhoels, Utesov, and other representatives of the arts were also invited since they were known to be lively and witty people to spend an evening with. And if you invited people "for Babel," they all came.

Babel had his own purely professional interest in Ezhov. It was through this man that Babel was trying to understand the things that were happening "at the very top."

By the winter of 1938 Ezhov's wife had poisoned herself. Babel thought the reason for her suicide to have been the arrest of someone close to her who often came to their home. But that may have only been the final straw. "Stalin can't understand her death," Babel told me. "His own nerves are made of steel, so he just can't understand how, in other people, they give out."

❀

DURING HIS FINAL YEARS Babel was incessantly driven to write. He told me: "I get up every morning with a desire to work and work. If something disturbs me, I get very angry."

And there was much that got in the way. Would-be writers, or graphomaniacs as we called them, were the worst problem. Babel was such a kind man that he was unable to be brutally frank, so he would avoid saying anything or be extremely vague. In the end he might say: "God's given you something to work with." Or: "There's discernible talent in your work, but it is still raw." The graphomaniacs would take heart, recast their work and be back at Babel's door. Others might be telling them to find something else to do, but Babel was encouraging them.

Also, there was the incessant ringing of the telephone. Working at home became harder and harder. Tormented, Babel started to dissemble. When he answered the telephone he would always talk in a woman's voice. He did it masterfully, too

— as I was to learn when I called home from work. And when our daughter Lida started talking, he would make her pick up the telephone and say: "Daddy's not home." But since this was never enough for her rich imagination, she would add something of her own, like: "He went for a walk in his new *kaloshes*."

To avoid the graphomaniacs, though, there were times when Babel would have to stuff a little suitcase with the manuscripts he needed and escape from home. He never missed a chance to rent a room that had come free for a month, or he might even stay in a hotel. Visits from my relatives provided another very infrequent reason for his flight. At those times, he would say to everyone with obvious pleasure, "Fair-haired gypsies have taken my castle — I must flee."

Material hardship also interfered with Babel's working. I only came to understand this during our last two years together. Initially he was very careful to keep me from knowing about his financial difficulties. He even told my mother when she visited, "We must always meet Antonina with a smile. Not a word about any household difficulties — her job is very demanding and she gets tired out."

Babel needed money not only to maintain our Moscow home but also to assist his mother and first daughter who were living abroad. It did not help matters that when Babel did have money, he would readily loan it out. Not only his friends but the most casual acquaintances exploited this character trait — and without bothering to pay him back. Because Babel was in constant financial need, he was forced to take some literary jobs just to earn money.

His work for the film industry served this purpose. Sometimes, he did the dialogue for an otherwise complete scenario, but more often he would revise an entire scenario or collaborate with a director in composing one from scratch.

Babel also retranslated the stories of Sholem Aleichem, which he felt had been rendered very poorly in Russian. And he did translations of works that no one had done before. I can remember his reading me one. It was a story about two Cossacks from Ukraine who are making porridge over a campfire out on the steppe. A tattered and hungry Jew wanders by. Wanting to have some fun, they invite him for porridge. The Jew accepts and they give him a spoon. But whenever the Jew lifts a spoonful of porridge to his mouth, one of the Cossacks takes his own spoon and hits the Jew in the head, saying, "Your Jew's eating more than mine; if he keeps it up, there'll be nothing left for my Jew." Then the other Cossack does the same, saying: "It's your Jew that's not leaving anything for mine to eat." And so they keep on beating the Jew, each pretending to be concerned for his own Jew while striking the other's.

As Babel put it, he worked on Sholem Aleichem to "feed his soul." Other "food for the soul" came from writing new stories and the novella "Kolya Topuz." He told me, "I'm writing a novella in which the main character is a former Odessa gangster like Benia Krik. His name is Kolya Topuz, and so far, at least, that's also the name of the novella. I want to show how this sort of man adapts to Soviet reality. Kolya Topuz works on a collective farm during the time of collectivization, and then he goes to work in a Donbass coal mine. But since he has the mentality of a gangster, he's constantly breaking out of the limits of normal life, which leads to numerous funny situations."

Babel spent a great deal of time writing, and he finished many works. Only his arrest prevented his new works from coming out.

In April 1939 Babel went off to Leningrad. He had been gone a few days when I received a telegram from I. A. Gruzdev.

"Babel has suffered a major asthma attack. Come immediately."

I had my doubts — was Babel playacting again? I recalled how once, when we were in Odessa in 1935, Babel had wanted me to stay an extra week and he had wangled a doctor's note from the hospital. I remembered sitting with friends in the Red Hotel café, discussing at length what illness was to strike me down. After many different ones had been nominated, someone suggested that I contract an inflammation of the inner ear. Everybody found it funny, so that was what I came down with. I used this note to justify returning late, but I did not submit it to the Comptroller. So, feeling dubious about Babel's illness, I showed the Gruzdev telegram to my boss, and he immediately gave me a few days off.

Babel, in high spirits and entirely healthy, met me in the Leningrad railway station accompanied by my friend Mariya Vsevolodovna Tyzhnova (Maka). When Babel had left for Leningrad I had given him a letter to take to Maka, and this had led to their becoming good friends. More than friendship was involved. Babel had a very special reason to visit her often. The maiden name of Maka's mother was Lermontov, and her father was a second cousin to Mikhail Yurevich Lermontov.*

Preserved in their very old home on the corner of Masterskaya Street and the Griboedov canal was a large room with carved cupids on the ceiling, a gold-framed mirror set between two windows and plaster mask of Peter the Great. Besides Maka, her grandmother, an aunt and her family, and her bachelor uncle, Vladimir Vladimirovich Lermontov, lived in this home.

From his talks with Vladimir Vladimirovich, Babel learned that the archive of an uncle of Lermontov's was kept there. Of

---

* Mikhail Yurevich Lermontov (1814–1841), Russian author.

Koltsov, Babel, Malraux, Gorky, 1936.

course, Babel wanted to look at it, so he visited regularly to read through the materials.

I remember Babel saying that Lermontov's uncle had been married twice and, in his diary, he had this to say about marriage: "Man's first wife comes from God, the second is of this world, and the third is the Devil's doing." After the death of his much loved first wife, Lermontov's uncle had ordered that the clock be stopped not only in his own lifetime but after his death as well. Babel read with interest the old expense ledgers of the Lermontov household, where the amount and the cost of firewood, hay, meat, candles, and such were recorded. Among the various entries Babel found the following: "One ruble — to the Jews on their wedding." He was highly amused by this, and, afterwards mentioned it frequently. The archive in question is now located in the Pushkin House.

During his stay in Leningrad Babel finished his work on the film scenario *The Old Square, 4 (Staraya ploshchad', 4)*, on which he had collaborated back in Moscow with the scenarist V. M. Kreps.

We spent several days together in Leningrad, where we visited I. A. Gruzdev. His wife, like me, came from Siberia, and for dinner she treated us to Siberian meat dumplings. We also spent time at Maka's, walked around the city, went out to Peterhof, and for three days in a row visited the Hermitage Museum between breakfast and lunch. Never since have I been able to get such a comprehensive view of the Hermitage collection as I did during those days with Babel. It was during this time, specifically April 20, that Babel wrote the following to his mother: "Whew! The weight is off my shoulders. I just finished a job — wrote a screenplay in twenty days. Now I should be able to 'live honorably.' I'll be leaving for Moscow on the evening of the 22nd. I've already been to the Hermitage, and tomorrow I am going to Peterhof. The end of my labors has coincided with the first days of spring, and the sun is out...I'm going for a walk after doing the work of the righteous..."

And on the 22nd of April, Babel wrote: "For a second day I've been out — and what's more, it's spring...Yesterday, I had dinner with Zoshchenko, then stayed up until the morning with my editor from the Gorky days of 1918.

"At dawn I walked along Kamenoostrovsky Boulevard, across the Troitsky Bridge, beside the Winter Palace, through the stilled and wondrous city. This evening I'm leaving."

Before moving to Peredelkino at the beginning of May 1939, Babel told me that he was planning to stay out there all the time and would only come to Moscow on special occasions. "I have to finish a book of new short stories by the fall. And that's what I'll call it — 'New Stories.' Then we are going to get rich."

We made plans for all of us to move out to the dacha at the end of May when the weather got warm. Work on the film scenario for *My Universities* was almost over, and shooting had already begun. "I feel I owe it to Gorky," Babel said. He had been involved to some degree or other with all the filming of Gorky's works — *Childhood*, *In the World*, and finally, *My Universities*. He told me, "I have my mind on other things right now, but Ekaterina Pavlovna asked me to keep an eye on these filmmakers to be sure they don't distort his work or do something in bad taste."

As he left for Peredelkino Babel said good-bye cheerfully, remarking: "I won't be returning to this house soon."

He asked me to bring Mark Donskoi and his assistants out to see him on May 15th, as it was Donskoi who was directing *My Universities*. We arranged for them to pick me up at Metroproject after work.

At the time, the only ones home besides me were our housekeeper, Shura, and Ester Grigorevna Makotinskaya, who took care of little Lida.

On May 15, 1939, at five o'clock in the morning, I was awakened by a knock on the door of my room. When I opened it, two men in army uniforms entered and said that they were searching for someone and that they needed access to the attic.

It turned out that four men had entered. Two climbed up to the attic and two stayed downstairs. One of them announced that they needed to see Babel, who could tell them where this person was, and that I should drive out to the dacha in Peredelkino with them. I got dressed and we set off. I was accompanied by two men in addition to the driver, who knew the way perfectly and did not once ask me for directions.

When we arrived at the dacha, I woke up the watchman and entered through the kitchen with the two men behind me. Hesitant, I stopped in front of the door to Babel's room. With a gesture one of the men ordered me to knock. I did so and heard Babel say, "Who's there?"

"Me."

Then he got dressed and opened the door. Pushing me away from the door, the two men walked right up to Babel and commanded, "Hands up!" Then they felt his pockets, frisking him for weapons. Babel kept silent.

We were ordered into another room — mine. There we sat down, huddling close together and holding each other by the hands. Talking was beyond us.

When the search of Babel's room was completed, they put all his manuscripts into folders and ordered us to put on our coats and go to the car. Babel said to me: "They didn't let me finish." I understood that he was speaking of his book "New Stories." Then, very low, he said: "Inform André." He meant André Malraux.

In the car, one of the men sat in back with Babel and me while the other one sat in front with the driver. "The worst part of this is that my mother won't be getting my letters," Babel said, and then he was silent for a long time.

I could not say a single word. Babel asked the secret policeman sitting next to him, "So, I guess you don't get much sleep, do you?" And he even laughed.

As we approached Moscow, I said to Babel, "I'll be waiting for you, it will be as if you've gone to Odessa ... only there won't be any letters ... "

He answered, "I ask you to see that the child not be made miserable."

"But I don't know what my destiny will be ... "

At this point, the man sitting beside Babel said to me: "We have no claims whatsoever against you."

We drove up to the Lubyanka prison and through the gates. The car stopped before the massive, closed door where two sentries stood guard.

Babel kissed me hard and said: "Someday we'll see each other ... " And without looking back, he got out of the car and went through that door.

I turned to stone, and I could not even cry. For some reason I kept thinking, "Will they at least give him a glass of hot tea? He can't start the day without it."

They drove me to our home on Nikolo-Vorobinsky where

the search was still going on. One of the men who had gone out to Peredelkino made a telephone call to report that Babel had been brought in. It was apparent that he was asked the question: "Did he crack jokes?" To which he answered, "He tried."

I asked for permission to leave so as not to be late for work. Permission was given, so I changed and left. Ester Grigorevna, who lived with us, managed to whisper to me that she had been able to move a few pieces of Babel's clothing into my closet to keep for him should he need them. Before I left, one of the NKVD men made a telephone call to ask how many rooms to leave me, one or two. Then, addressing his partner, he said: "The instructions are to leave her two."

Actually, this was rather remarkable for the times: I was being allowed to keep two separate rooms out of the three-room Moscow apartment for my little daughter and myself. At the time, however, I did not pay the slightest attention to this. Besides this information, I was given a telephone number for the NKVD's First Section where, if necessary, I could call.

They sealed Babel's room, took away his manuscripts, diaries, and pages with signed dedications that had been torn from his books.

Now, remembering the telephone conversations, turning over in my mind all the details of the search and arrest, I conclude that Babel even then, *beforehand*, had already been convicted.

Summoning all my strength, I worked at Metroproject all day long. I had to consult with project organizers at the Palace of Soviets to request DC-grade steel for the construction of the Paveletskaia-radial Station, which I was in charge of at the time.

Mark Donskoi and his associates, whom I was supposed to take to the dacha to see Babel that day, never came to Metroproject to call for me. Obviously, they already knew that Babel had been arrested.

When the working day was over, I made my way home and only then broke down. What had happened was terrible, though I could not imagine a bad outcome to it all. I knew that Babel could not possibly be guilty of anything, and my hope was that this was all a mistake, that *there* everything would be cleared up. But the very experienced Ester Grigorevna, who had already been through not just a husband's arrest but also a daughter's, made no effort to console me.

Later, I was to learn that Meyerhold* and Koltsov† had been arrested at almost the same time as Babel.

✻

IT WAS THE FEELING of being helpless that was the most awful part of the whole experience. Imagine the person you care about most being in trouble, and you can do nothing! I wanted to run to the Lubyanka and tell *them* what I know about Babel that *they* couldn't know. Again, it was the veteran, Ester Grigorevna, who saved me from that step.

It was a good thing I had my work and that I had Lida. I would come home, take her in my arms and, for hours on end, pace the room from corner to corner. Ester Grigorevna had to go home to do translations so that she could earn money for parcels to send to her own prisoners. That meant I had no adult companionship.

I wrote to my mother in Tomsk about everything and asked her to come and stay with me. When she arrived and began to

---

* Vsevolod Emilyevich Meyerhold (1874–1940), theater director and founder of the Meyerhold Theater; he was executed in prison.
† Mikhail Efimovich Koltsov (Fridlyand) (1898–1940), Russian-Soviet writer and journalist; was shot in prison.

take care of Lida, I started to work like someone possessed. I also took driving lessons just to keep from having any spare time on my hands.

Prisoners were not allowed visitors. All I could do was go once a month to drop off 75 rubles for Babel at a small window in a courtyard off the Kuznetsky Bridge. One stood in line to give the money, for which there was no receipt. The lines were long, stretching from the window to the street entrance and even beyond. I was always so downcast that I never noticed particular people. I did notice that the people came from the intelligentsia and that, although there were some men, most of those standing in line were women.

After Babel's arrest, no one telephoned me any longer — with one exception, Valentina Aronovna Milman, who was Ehrenburg's private secretary, and who called within a few days of Babel's arrest. She was afraid to see me at home, so we arranged to meet near the Bolshoi Theater, and she offered me money. I refused the money since I was still working, but this action of hers, so rare for its time, I have never forgotten. From that time on, and for many years after, she became one of my closest friends. It was only sometime later that I guessed that the money was being offered by Ehrenburg, since his secretary, who probably earned a modest wage, could never have offered me such a sum.

Babel had introduced me to Ehrenburg back in 1934. One evening Ilya Grigorevich had come to see Babel, whom he usually met not at our house but either at his own or in a café.

Neither during supper, nor afterwards, did Ehrenburg pay the slightest bit of attention to me. He smoked a cigar, dropped the ashes on his jacket, talked with Babel exclusively, and never looked in my direction. I was not accustomed to such treatment.

Usually, everyone that Babel introduced me to spoke with me, asked me questions, showed some kind of interest in me. This was attributable to my being a construction engineer involved with the building of the Moscow subway. For a woman to be an engineer at that time was something rare, and the construction of the subway was of interest to everyone.

But only with Ehrenburg was it different, and as hard as Babel tried to get him interested in me, telling him, for example, that I had worked in the construction of the Kuznetsk Metallurgical Factory, which Ehrenburg had written about in "The Second Day," nothing worked. He simply ignored me. Needless to say, I immediately conceived an intense dislike for Ehrenburg and, at future meetings, when he arrived, I excused myself after supper or lunch and went to my room.

At the time of Babel's arrest in May 1939, Ehrenburg had been abroad and only returned to Moscow in 1940. Valentina Aronovna told me that when Ehrenburg unpacked his suitcase, the first thing he pulled out was a book by Babel, lying right on top.

When I learned this I understood how much Ehrenburg cared for Babel and that caused me to change my feelings about him. At the time, Babel's books were being withdrawn from all the libraries, and even keeping them at home was risky.

Some two months after Babel's arrest, I began to be harassed by court officials. Babel had signed agreements with some publishing houses from whom he had received advances. In order to recover the advances, these publishers had decided to take legal action against me. One after another the court officials turned up not only to inventory the furniture that was left in the two remaining rooms but even my dresses. I had no idea what to do, so I decided to seek advice from our "very good friend," Lev Romanovich Sheinin, who was then working in the Prosecutor's office.

When he spotted me, he became very upset, even turning pale. Was this the same man who had spent so many evenings with us, often staying until daybreak? Was it the same man who had been so lavish in the compliments he paid to our home and to me, particularly? Once he had regained his composure, Sheinin asked me to wait in an adjoining room. A little later he entered the room accompanied by a man in uniform. He clearly felt that, for his own safety, he had better talk to me in front of a witness.

As he heard me out, Sheinin appeared to calm down when he saw that I had not come to ask him to intercede on Babel's behalf. Still, it was not Sheinin, but his companion, who advised me to telephone the First Section of the NKVD. When I got up to go, Sheinin suddenly asked me, "Why was Babel arrested?" I responded with an "I don't know," and left.

When I got home I decided I would finally use the NKVD telephone number that one of the agents had given me during the search for the first time. I called and reported on the inventory being made. The party on the other end of the line said, "Don't worry, they won't be coming any more." And, indeed, I never saw them again.

There would be another time that I had to telephone the NKVD. I had received a call from the local police in the Peredelkino area informing me of the theft of rugs in the dacha — one that had been in my room and another smaller one from Babel's room. It turned out that they had been stolen by the watchman's brother, who had come from Ukraine. He had been apprehended after he had sold the rugs, so they confiscated the 2,000 rubles he was carrying. The local police said that I should get this money. When I phoned the First Division of the NKVD, I was told, "Go and get the money."

I did not go right away, but waited perhaps a month. When I finally went, I learned that the local comptroller had been convicted of embezzling the money, for which he received a five-year sentence.

❋

JUST PRIOR TO THE CELEBRATION of the Anniversary of the October Revolution a young NKVD officer came by — I can't remember whether he phoned ahead or not. He asked me to give him trousers, socks, and handkerchiefs for Babel.

How fortunate we were that Ester Grigorevna had managed to transfer trousers to my room. There were also handkerchiefs and socks for him in my dresser. The handkerchiefs I scented heavily with my perfume and then gave everything to the officer. I so much wanted to send Babel a greeting from home, even if it was just a familiar scent.

My mother and I wondered what the possible significance of the officer's visit could be. It seemed to us that it was a good sign, a sign that conditions were improving for Babel.

I was able to get money to Babel from June until November, when I was told he had been transferred to the Butyrskaya Prison, where in the future I would have to take the money from now on. There, they accepted the money for November and December of 1939, but in January 1940 I was informed that Babel had been convicted and sentenced by the Military Tribunal.

A lawyer I knew arranged for me to meet with a procurator for the Military Tribunal, a gaunt, ascetic-looking general. After he had looked through some papers, he told me that Babel had been sentenced to ten years without the right to correspond and with the confiscation of all his possessions.

Before meeting with the general I had heard someone say that "ten years without the right to correspond" was euphemism intended for relatives that actually meant the person had been executed. I asked the general about this, assuring him that the truth would not cause me to faint. He said: "That does not apply to Babel."

After this visit with the Procurator for the Military Tribunal, I went to the NKVD reception office. I remember this as being on the second floor of a most unprepossessing two- or three-story building that used to stand where the Children's World department store was later built on Dzerzhinskaya Square. The general reception area was somber and led into a corner room where a card catalog stood. I was met by a young and unpleasant snub-nosed man who dug through the card catalog and then told me officially what I had already heard. And then he added, "A heavy sentence — you need to get your life in order." This angered me, so I said to him: "I have a job, how else am I supposed to put my life in order?"

He had bluntly hinted that Babel had been shot, but I was not about to accept it.

During the summer of 1939 I stayed with little Lida in Moscow the entire time. I could not leave on vacation to take her to a dacha; every day I was hopeful I might receive news of Babel. Rumors about his situation constantly surfaced in Moscow: someone had supposedly shared a cell with him, another person asserted that the state's case against Babel wasn't worth the paper it was written on, etc., etc. I tried to meet with these people but each time something prevented it. It would always turn out that the sources of the rumors had not themselves been in prison with Babel, but rather they knew people who had either left Moscow or were afraid to meet with me.

Once, during the summer the daughter of Esenin and Zinaida Raikh,* Tatiana, came to see me. She had heard that Babel and Meyerhold were sharing a cell, and she wondered if I might know something about their situation. I did not.

I took a real liking to Tatiana, who was strikingly blond with marvelous deep blue eyes. But it was not just her appearance that I found so attractive, it was also her willingness to go anywhere, even to the ends of the earth, to find out something about her stepfather Meyerhold, and to try to help him. I felt the very same way about Babel. But, having discussed all the rumors that were circulating and to what lengths we were futiley pursuing them, we parted company. I never saw Tatiana again, but I did hear about the rough fate she endured.

There was still another right that prisoners' families had: once every year they were entitled to go to an NKVD office at 24 Kuznetsky Bridge where they could make a formal inquiry about the fate of their imprisoned relative. Then, when they were officially notified, they could, at an appointed time, go back for the response. The inquiries had to be dropped into a special container outside the building, while the response was provided at a barred window within the building. In spring of both 1940 and 1941 I got the same response: "Alive in labor camp."

At the end of summer 1940 they came by to pick up Babel's possessions marked for confiscation. My brother, Oleg, was visiting me at the time, and Lida was living with her grandmother at a dacha I had rented near Kubinka Station along the Moscow-Belorussia railway line. The NKVD officer opened the sealed door to Babel's room, went into the dining room and, having

---

* Zinaida Nikolayevna Raikh (1894–1939), an actress and wife of the poet S. Esenin, later married to Vsevolod Meyerhold.

asked me to enumerate Babel's possessions, began to compose the list.

I was surprised when I heard my brother, Oleg, offer to help, to take down drapes, roll up the rug, bring Babel's suits and underwear. The NKVD agent was glad to have the help, but he was surprised to see us react so calmly, even in good spirits. This was because I had noticed when I entered the room that Oleg had cut the rug so as to leave me a huge part, and he had also switched the drapes. The drapes in my room were made of ordinary heavy material with a printed design, while Babel's were not only made from the finest cloth but were also lined and had a layer of flannel between the lining and the good side. When I noticed this switch I simply could not help laughing — and again I noticed the agent's surprise that we could be in such a good mood.

Also removed from the dining room was a beautiful, ornately carved, dark mahogany sideboard, an antique that Babel himself had bought from someone. Paintings and other lesser items were also removed, but a couch, as well as the dining room table and chairs, were left.

I hated to part with Babel's sofa-bed, which he had specially ordered, so I asked if the couch could go in its place, and the agent readily agreed. When the inventory was finished, some workers came and loaded everything into a truck.

Babel's room was again locked up and it remained empty for a long time. It was not until spring 1941 that an investigator from the NKVD moved in there along with his wife. For him we were not human beings, but enemies of the people. That was his only term for us. This magistrate had been educated as a mining engineer, but it was obvious that even while he was still at university he had been drafted into the Organs of the Secret Police and had never worked in his field of specialization.

With Isaac Leopoldovich Livshits.

I don't know what he did during the war but in all likelihood he disgraced himself, because soon afterwards the Organs fired him and he had to look for work. He found a job managing a tavern somewhere in Moscow. His friends would come with vodka and give him free drinks. And in his managerial position he had to entertain the regional party bosses and drink with them. And so he became an alcoholic and drank his way to oblivion. Twice the authorities threatened to confiscate his possessions as a penalty for his embezzling, but he would immediately have all his things carted off, so there would be nothing found to confiscate. In the end, he was fired from his job as tavern manager. He found a few other jobs, each one lower than the last, until he ended up working as a night watchman at a warehouse. But even there he was fired for drunkenness. His wife left him.

To live in the same apartment with him was not just difficult, it was revolting. Every day he would get drunk and pound on our door, or he would leave the door to the street wide open, or leave the gas burners on, or bring in all sorts of drunks from off the street. To fall asleep before he had gotten home was dangerous. Only when I heard him snoring would I get up and go downstairs, close the door to the street, turn off the gas burners and the lights, and then go to sleep.

And it was with a man like this that we were obliged to live for seventeen years in a communal apartment.

The legendary kindness of Russians towards drunks could be seen through the treatment our fellow tenant received. No matter where he might fall down drunk on the street, somebody would always drag him home. It might be a woman, or a young policeman, or a well-dressed man whose clothes would get thoroughly soiled in the process. They would bring him home, or call up and say: "Please come and collect your drunk." And there wasn't even one time when he got a cold or got sick, until at last he died of a heart attack one night on a kitchen table in the building next door.

When I learned of this the next morning, I was glad — that's how sick I had grown of life together with such a person.

This former magistrate lived in Babel's study for seventeen years, and never once did he have a book in there. In general, he never read anything. This was amazing to me, as the man had gone to school, graduated from an institute, and yet had not acquired any need at all to read. And in our Soviet land it was people like these who took the place of intellectual, educated, and talented people.

I really did not want to write about this, but I have yet to encounter memoirs that describe what everyday life was like for the families of the people arrested, even though I have heard it talked about a great deal. It illustrates another aspect of life during the cult of the personality.

❊

MY WORK AT METROPROJECT continued just as before. Most of my close colleagues did not know what had happened, and those who did never spoke of it.

In the fall of 1939 I was called before the Party Committee of the Metroproject and asked to work as a social activist in the Project's dormitories. When I said that my husband had been arrested, the Party Secretary responded calmly, "That has no bearing on your situation."

It has always been a mystery to me whether he said this on his own, or whether he had received directions concerning me from higher up. In any case, I did not detect any lack of trust, so like the rest of my colleagues, I ran community-service work on behalf of Metroproject. Moreover, I remained in charge of the group that was planning and designing the Paveletskaya-radial Station.

Metal materials for the Paveletskaya-radial Station were produced in Dnepropetrovsk. I had gone there previously on a number of business trips, but the one I made at the beginning of June was especially important. Our need for the materials had become pressing, but production was being held up at the factory.

As it turned out, the situation at the factory was complicated. A young man, arriving at the same time I did, was insisting that materials for bridge construction in the north be made top priority. Trying to convince me to agree to this, he said: "If we don't get these materials right away, we won't be able to get food to the prisoners in the camps." One can imagine the pain I felt upon hearing these words! I had no idea where Babel was imprisoned — maybe it was in one of these very camps.

Since he was concerned about the welfare of prisoners, I liked him right away. Alternating production and delivery dates, we worked out a compromise and reached a joint agreement with the factory.

I returned to Moscow on June 14th and on June 20th I left for Abkhaziya to take up an assignment involving the Sochi-Sukhumi railway construction, which included the building of eight tunnels. At that time Metroproject already had a planning contingent assigned to Novyi Afon, but it needed to be strengthened. At first I refused, because in the summer I was busy renting a dacha and moving Lida and my mother out of Moscow. But my superiors very much wanted me to go and suggested I take Lida and my mother with me, so I agreed.

The project involved securing the tunnel passageways, determining on site how to protect the tunnels against landslides, and rechanneling water. It was felt that our project team should be able to finish this task in four to six weeks, so we only took along summer clothing.

As our train was coming up on Lazarevskaya Station we found out that the war had started. A public meeting concerning it was being held right on the station platform. When the meeting was over and we had returned to the train, Lida said gaily, "Well, that's the end of the war."

Many of the passengers went directly back to Moscow from Sochi. We took the bus to Novyi Afon, and arrived in total darkness. A blackout had been ordered, as the Germans were bombing our cities.

For its work our project team occupied one large hotel room, and my colleagues lived in this same hotel. The management of tunnel construction was based in Gudauta, and railway construction was based in Sukhumi. Along with us in Novyi Afon we also had our own transportation office, which supplied us with trucks and cars.

Soon after we arrived, Novyi Afon became deserted. The vacationers who had been there left, and there were no new arrivals. The beaches were empty, and the resorts shut down.

We started work in the morning, often going out to see that the tunnels were being built according to specs, or going to meetings in Sukhumi and Gudauta. At first, I worked on tunnels 11 and 12 in the Myussersky Pass between Gagry and Gudauta. Sometimes, I had to stay overnight in Gagry's empty Hotel Gagripsh, where I would have to use a candle to get to my room. Memories of my stay there with Babel in 1933 prevented me from falling asleep. It was also difficult getting used to seeing the luxuriant Gagry utterly deserted. At least in Novyi Afon there were, besides the local population, the tunnel construction crews and the members of our project team. And some life was added by the comings and goings of our trucks, and the bosses would occasionally drive by in their cars.

Not one of the maps for the region was reliable, and as a result none of the tunnels that had been planned in Moscow actually fit the natural setting. Consequently, the work of our project team was much more demanding than projections had foreseen. All the calculations for the tunnel passageways had to be redone and new drawings made. Tunnels 15 and 16 in Eshery were partially located in landslide zones, so the plans for the areas adjacent to the openings had to be fundamentally reworked.

One end of tunnel 14 in Novyi Afon had been projected to come out on land where only recently a dacha for Stalin had been built. As a result, we had to change the route, forgo the use of a natural hollow, construct trestles, dig trenches, and, in short, make a minimal impact upon Stalin's plot of land, which was densely covered with lemon trees.

When it became evident that we had far more work to do than could be fit into our one-month assignment to Novyi Afon, and when our firm's Moscow operations were evacuated to Kuibyshev, the Chief Engineer for Metroproject, Abram Grigorevich Tankilevich, ordered us to stay where we were. None of us had brought winter clothes, so Moscow arranged to forward them. I did not have relatives in Moscow, so I sent our apartment key to my good friend Valentina Aronovna and asked her to pick up our clothes and take them to a collection point at Metroproject. My colleagues made similar arrangements.

Valentina Aronovna was still working as Ehrenburg's secretary, and when she gained access to our apartment, she had the good sense to take him the large rug from my room to warm the floor where he worked. She also took him the coffee maker Babel had brought back from Paris in 1933. I was glad to see these things be of some use to Ehrenburg, and, moreover, when we returned, we got them back, which is more than I can say about many items that our neighbors "borrowed."

The first year of the war went by almost peacefully for us in the Caucasus. Nevertheless, as the war dragged on, a number of my colleagues started feeling anxious and wanted to leave for Moscow. By that time the Germans had cut off rail connections between Sochi and Moscow. This meant having to go to Moscow via Kislovodsk, a trip that took forty days. Our group's director, B. V. Greitz, returned to Moscow with his wife. The trip was too long and dangerous for Lida, my mother, and me. I stayed behind as the group leader.

When we could no longer get cement from Novorossiisk we had to stop building the tunnels, so we were ordered to preserve them. For that we required lumber, and this necessitated our setting up timber processing operations near Pitsunda. Meanwhile, the Germans were approaching Tuapse. We immediately began to build a railway around the tunnels. Armaments were being shipped to Tuapse from Iran over a winding, extremely beat-up road. The road was ruined when the rains started, and the truck convoys stopped.

The Germans began bombing Tbilisi and Sukhumi. Their bombs were not particularly powerful, but there were casualties. One bomb fell near the administrative center for the railway and plaster rained down on the head of its director, A. T. Tsaturov. A woman engineer by the name of Rostomian raced out onto the square and lost a hand, and there was loss of life in other parts of Sukhumi. It was decided that the administrative center, responsible for the railroad construction, should move to Novyi Afon.

Then, German planes began flying over Novyi Afon. We would take cover in ditches that monks had dug long ago to divert water from the slopes of their olive groves. When our antiaircraft batteries fired at the Germans, the shell casings would fall down on us.

Possibly the Germans had learned that our soldiers were using the empty resort facilities to rest, or it's even possible they mistook the white frost-protectors on Stalin's lemon trees for army tents. In any case, the bombing continued and we were afraid to stay at the hotel any longer, so we found a room for rent and moved into a settlement called Psyrtskh.

Communications with Moscow were broken off, and I no longer received my salary. I had to do contract work with individual clients or with Abkhazian organizations. Our group built bomb shelters — a small one in the courtyard of the Regional Party Headquarters, a large one in the city proper.

The situation was becoming more and more alarming. The Germans had advanced to within five miles of Tuapse, and what was worse, they had taken up positions in the mountains above us, while our forces were retreating. There were times when several of our soldiers slept overnight on the floor of my room.

One morning my landlord, Arut Morgosovich Yanukian, pointed to the home of an Abkhazian stood right across from us. Overnight, a five-pointed star had been removed from its facade, but its trace was evident in the new wood underneath. Arut said, "He's expecting the Germans ... But don't you worry, I'll lead everyone off into the forest up in the mountains. I know of places that no German will ever find. We can sit things out there until our boys make it back."

Not completely reassured, I went for advice to our administrative director, Aleksandr Tigranovich Tsaturov. Quite apart from my mother and Lida, I had to be concerned for my remaining co-workers and their families. Tsaturov pointed to his desk and said, "Underneath the blotter I have a signed order from Kaganovich that instructs us to leave for Iran if things get dangerous. Remember, we have vehicles at our disposal."

Soon afterwards, the Germans who held positions up in the mountains were driven out by volunteer forces under the command of Red Army regulars. When we finished off the railway around the tunnels and the military equipment began rolling in, the Germans were thrown back from Tuapse.

Our military personel were enormously pleased to see the railway line completed. The meeting to mark its opening ended with hugs, kisses, and the builders being tossed in the air.

In reality, the railway was nothing to boast about. Ravines were bridged with rickety trestles; in the landslide areas it was necessary to spread gravel between the rails on a daily, never-ending basis, for it would immediately begin falling seaward. This Sisyphean labor was given to workers' brigades, comprised of felons who were not trusted enough to be sent to the front.

The situation in Novyi Afon improved and with it the mood of the populace. The news from the front was becoming more encouraging.

While staying at Arut's home, I often thought that if Babel was released but not allowed to live in Moscow, we could settle here, in this garden with a gazebo covered with grapevines and the magnificent view of the sea.

When 1944 arrived, it was time to go back to Moscow. Lida had turned seven and I had to consider her schooling. In Novyi Afon she was growing up to be a full-fledged country girl. In the morning she would use a special corn-picking rig to gather ears of corn, grind the kernels by hand, and go feed the chicks and the hens. The chicks got so tame around her that they would sit quietly on her head and shoulders as she paraded around the yard. In the evenings the shepherd would call out not to Olya, the mistress of the house, but to Lida: "Hey Lida, come get your cow." So Lida would take the rope down from the nail, run through the gates, wrap the rope around the cow's horns, and lead it back across the garden and into the cowshed. Lida was as comfortable in the sea as any Armenian or Abkhazian child. She could dive and swim just beautifully. She would swim so far out that one would lose sight of her, and she would stay out there for hours on end. If I had regularly witnessed these swims, my nerves would never have held out. Most of the time I heard about them after the fact.

We returned to Moscow in February 1944. The route home took us through Stalingrad, and while the train was making a stop, Lida and I went to the square. The sight of a city so completely destroyed was terrifying. In some places all that remained of a high brick building was the odd wall. Otherwise there was nothing to see but crushed brick. On the square in front of the railway station was a shell-shaped basin of a water fountain surrounded by sculptures of little children that had only been halfway reduced to rubble.

The rest of the way from Stalingrad to Moscow we repeatedly encountered sights of horrible destruction. While we had lived in Novyi Afon we had not really experienced the worst aspects of war, so these pictures of destruction on the way back to

Moscow gave me my only personal impressions of the war. To this day they remain vivid in my mind. In Moscow one occasionally saw signs of destruction, but mostly they were quickly cleared away, so this part of the war did not stand out.

Even though the State Defense Committee was supposed to have ensured the security of my apartment, it had been laid to waste. The tenants "lower down," together with the head of the military committee and the local chief of police, had spread the rumor that I, being the wife of an arrested enemy of the people, had gone over to the Germans and would not be returning. The Building Management Committee (BMC) had therefore given one of my rooms to a mason, and another was taken by the head of the BMC. There had been several of these committee heads during the war and, for some reason, each successive one had found it necessary to move into my room. Virtually all of my personal belongings had been removed.

Back at the end of 1943 a distant relation of Babel's, Mikhail Lvovich Poretsky, had left the front and come to Moscow. He went to the BMC and after explained that I was still away on assignment and would be returning soon. He then got control of one room when it came free — due to the departure of the head of the BMC. Poretsky padlocked the room and gave the key to the director of Metroproject, Robert Avgustovich Sheinfain, who met us at the train station. When we got to our room it was so cold that we could not stay there overnight. I had to place Lida and my mother with some tenants in another section of the building, and I was able to sleep over at a friend's house.

Poretsky had left a German stove for us with Babel's aunt. I hauled it home on a sled and once we got fuel for it, the room became livable. Except for the furniture, though, the place was bare — no dishes, no linen, blankets, pillows, etc. I was happy to find photographs lying in the wardrobe, some of them Babel's. But the most awful thing was that not a single book remained in the house.

It was going to take a good deal of money just to reacquire the bare essentials. I resumed working at Metroproject and took on the planning and design of the Kiev station stop, including any construction related to its connection to the subway radial line.

I tried to earn extra money by working evenings on any sort of construction design work that happened along. Since so much effort was going into restoring what had been destroyed, I had all the work I needed.

As a top personal priority I managed to find a woman who sold me her book collection, which contained one-volume sets of the major classics of Russian literature. I also went to second-hand bookstores and, whenever I came across titles that Babel and I had shared, I always bought them.

In order to get my other room back, I had to go to court. The laws were on my side. The apartment had been secured for me by an official order of the State Security Service and Metroproject. I had always paid the rent, and the mason had done likewise — his rent having been used by the BMC to fund a display of Marxist-Leninist saints and their sacred writings. Nevertheless, the People's Court ruled against me, and Judge Matrosov proclaimed: "I cannot bring myself to give a second room to such a small family when we have full-fledged generals who have been reduced to lying about in hallways." While I found his statement very touching, I could not agree to live three in a room. When I appealed, the City Court set aside Matrosov's decision, and our other room was returned to us. Chelnokov, the mason, was given back his former room and the two of us remained friends.

I was extremely fearful when, in the summer of 1944, I made the usual inquiry to the NKVD respecting Babel's fate. The reason for my trepidation? I had heard from acquaintances that the usual response from the NKVD was: "Died in 1941," "Died in 1942," and so on. And I dreaded hearing it. So I was delighted to receive a response that said: "Alive and well in camps." I received the very same response in 1945 and 1946, and the reply to my 1947 inquiry read: "Alive and well in camp; will be released in 1948." Our joy was boundless. My mother and I decided that there must have been a decision to grant Babel an early release.

During the summer of 1947, in anticipation of Babel's return, we had the apartment renovated and the furniture reupholstered. But, in the summer of 1948 a curt reply to my inquiry once again read: "Alive in camps." I decided this meant we had reached a stage of even greater arbitrariness and that Babel's sentence had probably been increased. Around this time rumors were rampant concerning longer sentences being meted out in the camps themselves, and with every sort of arbitrariness.

After 1948 I stopped making my annual inquiries to the NKVD. When 1952 arrived, there was still no sign of Babel. In August of that year my mother called me at work and said that I should come home immediately. I flagged down a taxi in the hope of finding Babel waiting for me at home. When I arrived, it turned out that we had had a visit from a former prisoner — a con or *zek* who perfectly fit the description that Solzhenitsyn was to provide for this type. He told my mother that he had been in a Kolyma camp since the war when he had been arrested for collaborating with the Germans. This got him an eight-year sentence, which he had now finished serving. He said his name was Zavadsky and that he came from Brest. He went on to tell

[135]

us that he had been transferred from camp to camp and that he had run across Babel. He said he did not have a letter from Babel, because his own release had allegedly come at a time when Babel was in the hospital. Zavadsky did pull out of his boot a letter addressed to a woman in which an inmate had written something about Babel. He told my mother her name — Mariya Abramovna — and he left us her telephone number. Zavadsky had been unable to wait for me, because he was in a hurry to catch a train. Mother said that Zavadsky, who was wearing an old worn overcoat and boots, looked haggard and that his complexion was gray.

I telephoned Mariya Abramovna and she invited me over. On the way to her place, I felt hesitant about going, for I was afraid of being followed. Maybe this explains my inability to remember exactly where she lived — I think it was on some lane between the Arbat and Gertzen Street. It was an old building in which the doors were massive and the ceilings high. A very pretty woman opened the door for me. Her black hair was combed flat, parted neatly down the middle, and gathered in a heavy bun at the back. Her facial features were classically symmetrical, her physique tall and somewhat full.

She told me that her husband (I vaguely remember her calling him Grisha, but I don't recall a surname) had served as an ambassador or an envoy to the U.S. She and her two daughters had been with him. Suddenly, in 1937 or 1938, he had been recalled to Moscow and they settled into a luxurious suite in the Hotel Metropol. For people in the foreign service, who were waiting to be assigned an apartment, being billeted at the Metropol was standard practice. That was where they came to arrest her husband just a few days after their return from the U.S. They arrested her, too, although I cannot remember if it was at the same time or later. At first, her daughters were

With Eisenstein, 1936.

hauled off to an orphanage, then they were placed with her parents. As best I can recall, she had somehow been released after a year or two. This was amazing in and of itself, but at the time I was not at all suspicious.

Mariya Abramovna told me how Zavadsky had come to see her, looking very fearful as he removed his boot to withdraw the letter. Then, climbing up on a chair to reach high up into a corner cupboard, she got the letter and read it to me. I asked her if she recognized her husband's handwriting and she said: "Well, yes and no. It looks like his writing, but it's as though his hand were shaking while he was writing." From the letter itself I remember verbatim the line: "How sad Babel will be when he leaves the hospital and finds that he missed the occasion to send a message home." Further on, it was mentioned that Babel was working as an accountant, that it was warm where they were, and that he was writing a great deal. Nothing much was made of his being in the hospital — his being discharged a certainty. I was struck by the word "occasion" *(okaziya)*, a Babelism he frequently used in his letters. I burst out crying, and so did Mariya Abramovna. We cried together for a while, but we had to face facts: what could we possibly do?

After this August 1952 meeting, neither of us ever contacted the other. I was certain that Babel was alive somewhere in Kolyma. I did have trouble understanding how someone as winsome as Babel could possibly fail to get word out to us from the camp. I could explain it, first of all, by the severity of the camp regimes and, secondly, by our nearly three-year absence from Moscow.

On the slight chance it might help, we decided to send an inquiry to the region of Magadansk. One of my friends found out where we should send our query. It was young Lida who wrote to P.O. AB 261 — the routing point for all the camps of Magadan and the region of Magadansk — and asked if they had an I. E. Babel staying there. The response read: "In answer to your inquiry, this is to inform you that there is no record of Babel, Isaac Emmanuilovich (b. 1894), in Magadan, region of Magadonsk — P.O. AB 261."

Another time I was informed that the writer K had told another writer, Evgeni Ryss, how Babel had died in a camp near the city of Kansk in the region of Krasnoyarsk. I tried to find Ryss, but he lived in Leningrad and I had no luck. Then in 1955, after Babel had already been rehabilitated, K himself phoned me and said that if I cared to hear the details concerning Babel's death, he would meet with me. We met on Tverskoi Boulevard across from Gertsen House.

K informed me that his father had been the warden of the camp near Kansk. The inmates worked with sewing machines, and they had made Babel a dark-green canvas cloak, which he wore regularly. K said that this cloak was now being kept by his mother in Siberia, but if I wanted it he would get it for me. Babel had his own room in this camp; they did not force him to work, so he was able to write.

"I was the one who got him his writing paper," K said. "I was working for a newspaper in Vladivostok. My father liked Babel a great deal. He would write me and say Babel needed paper, and I would send it. One day Babel went into the yard for a walk wearing that cloak of his, and after a while we noticed he had been gone a long time. We were all worried, so we went out to look for him. There was a lone tree growing in the yard and next to it there was a bench. Babel sat on the bench leaning against the tree. He was dead."

So much for Babel's whereabouts — a garment-maker's shop in a camp near Kansk.

I did not insist on K's getting me the cloak. It was not that I suspected anything, it was just that I was frightened at the thought of keeping it in the house.

It was during the May Day festivities a year or two after this meeting with K that a girlfriend and I went for a rest to the Composers' Home near Ruza. While out for a walk, we stopped off at a building set aside for writers and there we ran into Evgeni Ryss. After we had been introduced, I asked him if K had told him about Babel's death, and, if so, could he repeat for me what he had been told.

K had told Ryss that his father was, indeed, the warden of the Kansk prison where Babel was serving his sentence. The warden's quarters were right next to Babel's cell and both shared a common balcony. Babel used that balcony for frequent visits to K's parents. K's mother would make meat dumplings for Babel. It was on their black vinyl sofa that Babel had died of a heart attack. I again heard how Babel had spent much time writing and that K had supplied him with paper. Ryss also told me that after Babel's death an operative from the NKVD central office had come and taken his manuscripts to Moscow.

*

APPROXIMATELY A YEAR BEFORE Babel's arrest I first encountered Y. E. Elsberg when I got home after work. I was not at all surprised to find Babel with a new acquaintance. It wasn't the first time and, besides, Elsberg worked with Kamenev* at the "Academya" Publishing House. I was surprised, and amused, by Elsberg's readiness to get involved in all sorts of undertakings on our behalf. All I had to do was

---

* Lev Borisovich Kamenev (Rosenfeld) (1883–1936), Soviet statesman and Party leader, an aide to Lenin, was executed under Stalin.

mention that the apartment might need some sort of refurbishing and, the next thing I knew, he would bring painters by. If I mentioned that a plug had gone bad, an electrician would show up the very next day. One time Babel told me that Elsberg was going to take me to the Bolshoi Theater for a new staging of Glinka's *Ivan Susanin*. Elsberg hardly listened to the music and, before the end of Act I, he went off somewhere and came back with a bag of oranges for me. During Act II he left to order us a car, and, before Act III was over he left our box to bring us our coats. After the premiere, Elsberg took me home in a stylish black car. Back at the house I told Babel with amusement how Elsberg had looked after me at the theater.

While I know that Babel had been warned about Elsberg's having been assigned to watch him, I do not know how Babel viewed the situation. All I do know is that Elsberg kept coming to see us right up until Babel's arrest, and afterwards he came to see me regularly once a month. He would come by all dressed up like a suitor, bring children's books for Lida, have a glass of tea, and then leave. He never asked any questions and he never steered our conversations into political danger zones. I termed Elsberg's visits "courtesy calls." After every one of them a sense of confusion made me feel like shrugging my shoulders. Toward the end of 1939, Elsberg stopped visiting.

When those who had been "suppressed" were beginning to be rehabilitated, Elsberg's role became clear and there was talk of putting him on trial. A special commission was established to look into Elsberg's participation in the arrests of certain writers, and this commission was allowed to examine the cases against those writers. Of course the commission members had to formally swear to secrecy with respect to the details of the cases. Still, some information leaked out.

Elsberg was expelled from the Writers' Union and it was believed that he should be made to face criminal charges, but the authorities refused to allow this. After he had been discovered, I ran across him once at the Institute of World Literature. He looked so miserable that I responded to his nod of recognition, but I did not stop to talk. His was a miserable fate and a terrible life!

❋

I WAS AMONG THE FIRST to learn that prisoners were eligible for rehabilitation.

It so happened that the Chief Engineer for the Moscow Subway Project, Abram Grigorevich Tankilevich, along with his colleagues from the Railway Research Institute, were being tried on the basis of trumped-up charges. Tankilevich was not imprisoned, but he was placed under house arrest, so he had to make daily trips to attend the trial. Given the large number of people indicted, the trial was a long, drawn-out affair. Once, during a break in the proceedings, Tankilevich happened to overhear some lawyers talking and from this he learned of a Rehabilitation Commission presided over by the USSR's Attorney General Rudenko. This commission was to deal with the cases of people who had been condemned during the cult of Stalin.

It was in January 1954 that Tankilevich learned of the Commission, and he immediately telephoned to tell me what he had learned. I had heard nothing about such a commission, and I had no idea how one was supposed to approach it, but I immediately wrote up the following declaration:

My husband, the writer, I. E. Babel, was arrested on May 15, 1939 and sentenced to ten years in prison without the right to correspond.

According to documents I received annually from the Office of Internal Affairs, Babel is alive in a prison camp.

Considering Babel's literary talent, as well as the fact that it has been 15 years since his arrest, I am requesting that you re-examine his case with a view to a possible improvement of his lot.

A. Pirozhkova
January 25, 1954

In further correspondence addressed to Rudenko, I explicitly requested Babel's rehabilitation, but the first time I wrote him, that term was not in my vocabulary. Ten days after my next letter, and much to our amazement, we received a reply from Rudenko:

Your complaint of 5 February, 1954, addressed to the Attorney General of the USSR and concerning I. E. Babel, has been forwarded to the Chief Military Procurator and it is being examined.

You will be informed of the results.

Two weeks later, on February 19, 1954, we again received a letter from the USSR's Office of the Attorney General.

This is to inform you that your complaint is being examined by the USSR's Office of the Attorney General. The results will be conveyed to you under separate cover.

The first letter was signed by the Chief Military Procurator, the second one by the Procurator for Special Investigations.

But then months went by, until sometime around June a stranger telephoned and identified himself as Inspector

Dolzhenko. He invited me to come and see him. The Procurator's Section where Dolzhenko received me was located on Kirov Street not far from the Kirovsky Gate.

Dolzhenko was a likable middle-aged man. Leafing through a folder, he started out by asking about me — where I work, what I do, what sort of family I have. When he heard that I worked as Chief Engineer in the Subway Division of the Transport Department, he said, "Given the facts of your biography, I find that surprising."

The questions about Babel touched on his having been acquainted with Ezhov and André Malraux. I asked Dolzhenko:

"Have you looked over Babel's file?"

He replied, "I've got it right here."

"And what's your opinion?"

"It was a total fabrication."

At this point I nearly fainted. My vision dimmed and it was only by clinging to his desk that I avoided falling off my chair. Dolzhenko became very alarmed, jumped up and hurried over to me with a glass of water.

I quickly regained my self-control. Dolzhenko then asked who, among Babel's acquaintances, might be expected to provide a positive reference for Babel. I mentioned Ekaterina Pavlovna Peshkova, Ehrenburg, and Kataev.

Just imagine, the case against Babel was admitted to have been "a total fabrication," and yet it took three references to rehabilitate him.

Dolzhenko then said that, since it was summer and the people with whom he had to speak might be at their dachas or off on a trip, he could not promise a speedy resolution.

I inquired about Babel's fate and Dolzhenko responded that he was only involved in rehabilitation; a response to the question of Babel's fate would come from another source once he had finished his examination of the matter.

From Dolzhenko's office I immediately went to see Ekaterina Pavlovna Peshkova who lived nearby on Chaplygin Street. I had never just dropped in on her, so she was very surprised to see me. But the way I looked was such that she put her arms around me at once, led me into the dining room, sat me on the sofa, and sat down next to me. For a while I was unable to say anything. Then I told her about my talk with Dolzhenko and warned her that he might pay her a visit.

That same evening I called Ehrenburg and was told that he was out at his dacha and that a car would be going out there early the day after next. When I arrived at his dacha it turned out that Dolzhenko had already been there. Lyubov Mikhailovna spoke of how she had made Dolzhenko cool his heels in the garden for two hours — Ehrenburg had been busy.

"If I had known that he had come about Babel, I would have let him see Ilya Grigorevich at once."

Ehrenburg told me about his conversation with Dolzhenko. He said that it was he who had introduced Babel to André Malraux when they were in Paris together; he explained Babel's acquaintance with Ezhov as being driven by professional curiosity, the same kind of curiosity that he had about the men who drove the trotters at the racetrack.

I asked Ehrenburg what he thought Babel's fate might be. He replied, "His rehabilitation prospects look good — his fate, I'm afraid, the opposite."

In spite of my best efforts, I burst out crying. Ehrenburg immediately tried to assure me that he was only conveying his own impression, and that Dolzhenko had not said anything definite. He grabbed me by the hand and dragged me off to look at his flower bed where he was growing unusual and, for me, unfamiliar plants from seeds he had gotten during his travels abroad.

I did not try to alert Kataev about a visit from Dolzhenko, but I know that the two of them met. Dolzhenko also met with Ekaterina Pavlovna the very day after I had been to see her. From her Dolzhenko heard how fond she and Gorky had been of Babel, and how they considered him to be an exceptionally bright man and a gifted writer.

Dolzhenko repeated his surprise that I held a "lofty position" in the face of so much that was negative in my personal biography.

It was late in December before Dolzhenko telephoned to say that Babel's case was finished and that the Military Collegium on Vorovskaya Street could issue me a document confirming the rehabilitation. This is how the document read:

> The case involving Babel, Isaac Emmanuilovich, was reviewed by the Military Collegium of the USSR on December 18, 1954.
>
> In accord with circumstances just brought to light, the verdict of January 26, 1940 concerning Babel, I. E., is set aside and the case against him is quashed due to an absence of criminal evidence.

After reading this, I asked what had happened to Babel. The man who had just given me the document picked up a pen and wrote the following on a newspaper that was lying on his desk: "Died of cardiac arrest, March 17, 1941." He let me read it, then tore it from the newspaper and ripped it into shreds, saying: "You can get the official notice of death from your local Registry of Official Acts."

I left him feeling almost calm. I simply did not believe him! If it had said: "Died in 1952" or some year thereafter, I would have been convinced. But in August 1952 the inmate Zavadsky had brought that letter that read: "How sad Babel will be when he leaves the hospital and finds that he missed the occasion to send a message home." I believed Zavadsky and so I was convinced that until August 1952 Babel had been alive in a camp somewhere in Central Kolyma. I concluded that our secret police had too many prisoners to keep track of, so I immediately began an all-out search for Babel.

I wrote to Shcheptsov, the Chair of the Military Collegium of the Supreme Court of the USSR, who had signed the rehabilitation document and, at the same time I wrote to Serov, Head of the KGB. My letters stated:

On December 23, 1954 I went to the office of the Supreme Court of the USSR where I was given a document (No. 4n-011441/54) confirming that, due to the absence of evidence of criminal wrongdoing, the case against my husband, the writer, Babel, Isaac Emmanuilovich, was dismissed.

At the same time I was informed that, on March 17, 1941, my husband — Babel, I. E. — had died of cardiac arrest.

I believe this information to be wrong, for until 1948, the official oral replies to our family's inquiries addressed to the Information Office of the Ministry for State Security, 24 Kuznetsky Bridge, stated that Babel was alive in the labor camps. That I was repeatedly so informed from year to year completely contradicts the December 23 communication that Babel, I. E., died in 1941.

Furthermore, in summer 1952, I was visited by a prisoner released from a camp in Central Kolyma, who informed me that

Babel was alive and well.

Therefore, I am utterly convinced that Babel was alive until summer 1952 and that the news of his death is erroneous.

I am requesting that you use all available means to locate Babel, Isaac Emmanuilovich, that you inform me of his whereabouts, and that I be authorized to go and bring him back.

When I failed to get a response to these requests, I wrote the following to the writer Fadeev:*

Dear Aleksandr Aleksandrovich:

I am turning to you at the suggestion of Ilya Grigorevich Ehrenburg from whom you have probably learned about the complete rehabilitation of my husband, I. E. Babel.

Along with the rehabilitation document I received a verbal message that my husband had died in 1941. This message is erroneous, because I have it on good authority that he was still alive as of summer 1952. In August of that year I was sought out by a former inmate of a Central Kolyma camp who told me that for three years (1950–1952) he had been in the camp with I. E. Babel. What is more, he related a number of indisputable facts about Babel.

In view of the foregoing, I am extremely distressed over a situation that has seen the Military Collegium of the Supreme Court of the USSR exculpate Babel, yet do nothing to locate him, because he is thought to have died.

In a declaration sent to the Ministry for State Security I have disputed Babel's alleged death, but I fear that the MSS handling of the matter will be protracted and purely formal. Consequently, it is imperative that someone high up in government see that an

* Aleksandr Aleksandrovich Fadeev (1891–1956), Russian-Soviet writer and from 1939 headed the Union of Soviet Writers.

immediate search for Babel be initiated. One of the people who might do this is Voroshilov, who certainly knew Babel and remembers him.

It would be difficult for me to secure a meeting with Voroshilov, so I am hereby asking if you or the Soviet Writers Union will assist me.

Please let me know if you can help with the process of determining what has happened to Babel.

After getting my letter, Fadeev telephoned when I was not at home and told Lida that he would like to talk to me, but that he was on his way to Barvikha for a vacation, so he would get back to me after his return.

When I did not hear from Fadeev, I wrote to Voroshilov,* and somewhat later someone from his office called to give me the following message: "Kliment Efremovich has asked me to tell you that you should believe that Babel is dead, for, had he been alive, he would have been home long ago."

It was only after receiving this message that, while still dubious, I went to the local Registry of Official Acts to see if I could get an official record of Babel's death. It is hard to imagine anything more frightening than the document I received: *Place of death — Z; cause — Z.*

According to the document, Babel had died in March 1941 at the age of 47.

Was this a credible date? If Babel's sentence had been handed down on January 26, 1940 and if he was to be shot, it was impossible that his execution would have been delayed for over a year.

---

* Kliment Efremovich Voroshilov (1881–1969), headed the Red Army from 1925–1940.

I did not believe in this date either — and rightly so. In 1984 the Political Publishing House issued a calendar with tear-off sheets on which the one for July 13 read: "90 years since the birth of the writer, I. E. Babel (1894–1940)." When I phoned to ask why they had shown the year of his death as 1940, when the official record showed 1941, they calmly replied, "We got our date from official sources."

Why was it necessary to have the official record show that Babel died over a year later than was actually the case? Who found it necessary that I be deceived for so many years with official messages that he was "alive in the labor camps"? Who set up the Zavadsky visit and then forced the writer K to spread false rumors about Babel having died a natural death after a comparatively bearable existence in some camp or prison?

It was only when Babel's sister from Brussels visited us in 1960 and asked, "How did my brother die?" that I could understand how monstrously unthinkable it would be to say, "He was shot in prison." And so I too gave her one of the K versions that had Babel dying of natural causes in a labor camp while sitting on a bench next to a tree.

I did not want to believe in Babel's death, but from that point on, I ceased trying to locate him.

❉

WE NOW KNOW THAT Babel was tortured during his interrogation and that he held out, denying everything, for three days. As subsequent examples have shown, there were strong and brave people who were capable of enduring torture, but when those arrested were told that their wife and small child would be brought in and tortured right before their eyes, it must have been beyond anyone's endurance. In order to avoid that, Babel

Babel in 1934.

agreed to sign whatever accusations they set before him, which is to say, he signed his own death warrant.

But why his torments, even if only for three days, if he was doomed all along? To write of this is very hard for me. The anguish of loss never leaves me, and the thought that for eight months in an NKVD prison he had to endure a mass of insults, humiliation, and torture, and that his last day on earth was lived with the knowledge of his impending execution — all of this tears at my heart.

Everyone dies, but not so young unless it be from illness — often unexpected — but Babel was not even forty-six-years old. He was healthy, he loved life, he loved his work, and even in an NKVD prison, he had asked his investigators to give him his manuscripts so that he could continue to correct them — but that too was denied him.

I tried to locate Babel's manuscripts. When I made a formal request concerning this to the Ministry for State Security, I was summoned to a storage area that was half underground where an NKVD major told me, "In the registry of things taken from Babel there is, indeed, mention of five folders with manuscripts. I have personally looked for them, but with no success."

The major then handed me a piece of paper intended for the Comptroller's Office where I could be compensated for anything unlawfully taken. Neither Babel's things nor financial compensation held any meaning for me. But the manuscripts were another matter entirely. Consequently, for the first time, a full year after Babel's rehabilitation, I turned to the Writers' Union, and specifically, to its Secretary General, A.A. Surkov. I asked him to see that a search for the manuscripts be conducted in the name of the Writers' Union.

The following letter was sent to the Chairman of the KGB (the successor to the NKVD), General Serov:

In 1939, comrade I. E. Babel, a well-known Soviet writer, was arrested by the state security forces and subsequently condemned to death.

I. E. Babel was posthumously rehabilitated by the Soviet Supreme Court in 1954.

When he was arrested, Babel's manuscripts, personal archive, correspondence, photographs, and other such materials were confiscated. These have significant literary value.

Among the confiscated literary materials were five folders, which specifically contained: a collection of stories entitled *New Stories*, the novella, *Kolya Topuz*, translations of stories by Sholem Aleichem, diaries, etc.

The writer's widow, A. N. Pirozhkova, has tried unsuccessfully to retrieve the aforementioned materials from the relevant archive.

I am hereby requesting that you order a fully thorough search for the missing materials of the writer I. E. Babel.

> General Secretary
> Soviet Writers' Union
> *A. Surkov*

This letter received a swift reply stating that the manuscripts had not been found. It was really the same reply I had received, but the speed with which it came indicated that there had been no further search.

I began to suspect that Babel's manuscripts had been burned. When this has happened, responses about their status might state: "Manuscripts burned in accordance with no. such & such order to incinerate." This was the case when Boris Efimov inquired about the manuscripts of his brother, Mikhail Koltsov.

It was not until 1970 that I was visited by the young woman who worked for TSGALI, the central literary archives of the USSR. (I had decided to donate some of Babel's surviving manuscripts to them.) This woman assured me that manuscripts belonging to authors who had been arrested were still turning up. Sometimes they came from private sources, sometimes from the KGB archives. She allowed me to hope that, someday, Babel's manuscripts will also surface

I told her: "If they'd let me look for them in the KGB archives, I'd spend the rest of my days hunting for them."

"I would, too," she exclaimed passionately.

I was truly moved to hear this from the very young TSGALI archivist.

Still, I must admit that, at this stage, I can no longer hold out any hope that Babel's manuscripts have survived.

In 1987, when so much was changing in our country, I again made an official request that the KGB search for Babel's manuscripts in its underground storage areas. In response to my request I was visited by two KGB agents who informed me that the manuscripts had been burned.

"And so you've come in person to avoid giving me a written response to my request, am I correct?"

"How could you think such a thing? We came here to commiserate. We understand how precious Babel's manuscripts would be."

✽

WHEN THE WRITERS' UNION set up a commission to look after the literary legacy of I. E. Babel, I began receiving some manuscripts of his early works, as well as some first editions of his books. From both the Lenin Library and the Library of History I got photocopies and typescripts of early journal versions of his publications. Some of these I obtained on my own, but for the most part I received them from young scholars who, following Babel's rehabilitation, had begun writing dissertations on his works.

The first young man to do so was Izrail Abramovich Smirin, then Sergei Nikolaevich Povartsov, then Janina Salajczyk from Poland, and then others.

From Kiev, Tatiana Osipovna Stakh sent me Babel's Red Cavalry diary, some outlines for stories, a notebook of Babel's, and the manuscripts for some stories he had begun — "At Grandmother's" *(U babushki)*, "Three O'clock in the Afternoon" *(Tri chasa dnya)*, "There were nine of them" *(Ikh bylo deviat')*. Tatiana Osipovna had gotten them from M. Y. Ovrutskaya, at whose home Babel would occasionally stay when he was in Kiev.

Manuscripts for Babel's stories, "My First Fee" and "Kolyvushka," are being kept in Saint Petersburg by the son of Olga Ilinichna Brodskaya, to whom Babel had given them.

Gradually, a modest Babel archive has come in existence. Throughout the postrehabilitation years it has provided working material for scholars from many different countries.

The commission set up to look after Babel's literary legacy was comprised of: K.A. Fedin; L.M. Leonov; I.G. Ehrenburg; L.I. Slavin; G.N. Munblit; S.G. Gekht, and me.

Almost immediately after the establishment of the Commission it became obvious that neither Fedin nor Leonov wanted to actually do anything for it. As Chairman of the Commission, Fedin would receive letters with questions concerning Babel and he would forward these to me, unread.

Ilya Grigorevich Ehrenburg became the commission's *de facto* chairman. I used to turn to him for advice, particularly when consideration was being given to publishing works that had not appeared since 1936. We met fairly often during the negotiations surrounding the publication of a one-volume edition of Babel's selected works (*Izbrannoe*) for which Ehrenburg wrote an introduction.

On one occasion when we were to meet with the editor of the one-volume edition, we assembled outside the office of the associate chief editor for the Khudozhestvennaia literatura Publishing House. By "we" I mean Ehrenburg, Munblit, Gekht, Slavin, and myself. We were sitting on a sofa in front of the stairway leading up to the second floor. Gekht and Slavin were the last to arrive, and Slavin informed us that Fadeev had committed suicide. I looked at Ehrenburg. He did not seem in the least bit disturbed, and then said, "Fadeev had no other recourse. He was under siege from all those returning prisoners and their wives. The returnees wanted to know how it was that a personal letter sent to Fadeev could wind up on the desk of an investigator during their interrogation. And that is a good question, isn't it? After all, Fadeev himself was not arrested, his manuscripts were not confiscated. So didn't he have to be the one who volunteered the incriminating material?"

I was struck by the indifferent way the commission members met the news of Fadeev's suicide. No one seemed surprised or saddened in the least.

At the scheduled time we went upstairs to see the associate chief editor, who, after seating us, summoned the person who was to edit the Babel volume. A tall, buxom woman with a lovely Russian face came into the room. Her long earrings made a metallic sound, and the sleeves of her white blouse were rolled up. I glanced over at Ehrenburg, who seemed to have frozen in astonishment. When Munblit and I exchanged glances, it was all we could do to keep from laughing — not at the woman, of course, but at Ehrenburg. After we had been introduced and had finished talking over the contents of the book, we went back onto the street, where Ehrenburg said, "If a woman like that were to bring us a boiling samovar, I wouldn't be at all surprised. But should she be editing Babel?"

As the book was nearing completion, G.N. Munblit, who put together the commentaries for it, said to me: "I get heartburn whenever I talk to her."

My own relationship with the editor was fine except for one time when she said: "I think we should leave out 'The Cemetery in Kozin' (Kladbyshche v Kozyne) from Red Cavalry. It's a short piece that really doesn't have anything to offer." I almost blew up, but restraining myself, I talked her into keeping that amazing little masterpiece. For this edition, we proposed publishing "My First Fee," "Cow-Wheat," (Yvan-da-Marq), "Gapa Guzhva," and "Kolyvushka," but we were turned down. Ehrenburg was furious, but he said: "The day will come when they publish everything, but for now it's good at least this volume will appear."

Ehrenburg also advised me concerning the compilation of the 1966 one-volume edition of Babel's writings. While we managed to include some stories that had been excluded in 1956, "My First Fee," "Gapa Guzhva," and "Kolyvushka" were still rejected again. We also managed to bring out some of Babel's memoirs, some of his speeches, and a modest number of letters.

Once someone from the journal *Krugozor* called and asked me for something of Babel's. Ehrenburg encouraged me to give them something, an article or two that Babel had published during 1922 in the newspaper *Zaria vostoka*. We chose "Without a Homeland" and "At the Rest Home." Then the editors asked me to get Ehrenburg to write a brief introduction. Ehrenburg responded by saying: "Fine, I'll write that with these articles Babel became a full-fledged writer, and as for his first honorarium, the readers could find out about that from the story 'My First Fee.' It was a story no one dared publish at the time."

In 1957 Lyubov Mikhailovna called to tell me that Ehrenburg wanted to meet my daughter, Lida, so he was inviting us over. By then Lida was already twenty and studying at an architectural institute. After they had met, Ehrenburg said: "To be frank, when I heard that Babel had a daughter who looked like him, I was horrified. Babel's looks were fine for a well-known middle-aged author, but for a young woman to look like him? But it turns out she looks like him and is good-looking too."

After seating us, Ehrenburg took a seat directly opposite and began talking about Babel and about their encounters in Paris. Sometimes Lyubov Mikhailovna would interrupt and this would anger Ehrenburg. Or, if Lyubov Mikhailovna was talking and Ehrenburg thought of something to interject, then she would get angry. Lida, who had inherited her father's powers of observation, picked all this up remarkably well. Afterwards, she also could describe in minute detail what

Ehrenburg was wearing — what kind of jacket, tie, the pattern on his socks, and so on.

When Ehrenburg celebrated his seventieth birthday in 1961 he asked me to bring Lida along to the party, saying: "I'd like there to be at least one young face among my guests." He took pride in introducing her to his guests, who included Kaverin, Kozlovsky, Sarra Lebedeva, Slutsky, and many others.

The year 1964 marked the seventieth anniversary of Babel's birth. At Ehrenburg's prompting the commission in charge of looking after Babel's literary legacy sent the following letter to the Communist Party Central Committee :

The Executive of the Soviet Writers' Union has decided to commemorate the seventieth anniversary of Babel's birth. One feature of this decision will be the organization of a special commemorative evening at the Writers' House. The auditorium there can only partially accommodate those Moscow writers who might wish to attend. There is such enormous reader interest in Babel that we believe it unwise to restrict attendance to the confines of the aforementioned auditorium. We are hereby requesting that you help us get approval for organizing a second *public* evening in the Polytechnic Museum, during which there would be readings of Babel's works and people who knew Babel would recount their experiences with him. We feel certain that you will accommodate us here.

Ilya Grigorevich proposed that the letter also be signed by Fedin, who was the *de facto* chairman of our commission. With this in mind, Ehrenburg wrote Fedin as follows:

Dear Konstantin Aleksandrovich:

I am sending you the text of a letter the Babel Commission has decided to address to D. A. Polikarpovich. I am appealing to you both on a personal level and in your capacity as Chairman of the Commission to place your signature at the top of those signing on behalf of the Commission. I am certain you will agree to this.

Sincerely yours,
Ehrenburg

Fedin did not sign the letter, and replied he did not see any need to propose an extra evening at the Polytechnic Museum. Fedin's response made Ehrenburg angrier than I ever saw him before.

We were correct in our presupposition that the Writers' House would not hold all those who wanted to attend. Before the evening got underway, Gertsen Street, where the Writers' House was located, was overflowing with people. I was accompanying Ekaterina Pavlovna Peshkova, and even though we arrived early, it was all we could do to squeeze through the crowd to get to the entrance. The auditorium was jammed, and the lobby was full too. All the doors from the auditorium to the foyer were wide open so that those who could not be seated might still be able to hear. Nikolai Robertovich Erdman later told me that he had stood through the whole evening out in the lobby.

We had originally thought that Ehrenburg would be the master of ceremonies, but the Writers' Union had other ideas, and it named Fedin as the M.C. All the other Commission members were exasperated and upset. And we did not know how Ehrenburg would take this. What if he decided not to come? He did come, although he did not sit on stage, but rather took a seat in the front row. I did the same.

Fedin spoke first, and after him the writers Nikulin, Bondarin, Slavin, Lidin, and Munblit. Ehrenburg was the last to speak. I will cite certain parts of his speech from the written record:

While others have already spoken very well about Isaac Emmanuilovich, and while I have already written about him, I just had to take advantage of this forum too. Babel was the best friend I ever had. He was three and a half years younger than I, but I used to jokingly call him "the wise rabbi," because he was a genuinely wise man. Indeed, the depth of his understanding was amazing.

Babel was truly a kind and good man — not in the vulgar or bourgeois sense, but in the literal meaning of these words. And when it was said that Babel did not believe in the success of writers who had little concern for their spiritual integrity — that fully captured Babel's real nature.

Once I was late showing up for a meeting with him in Paris, so while he waited for me, he read a short story by Chekhov. When I showed up, he said to me: "You know what I find surprising? Chekhov was a very kind man."

Babel used to get into heated arguments with French people who were critical of one or another aspect of Maupassant's writing. He would argue that Maupassant was perfect. In one of our last conversations he said: "Everything that Maupassant wrote came out fine, but he lacked heart." Babel had sensed a streak of terrifying loneliness and isolation in Maupassant.

Babel could be extremely cautious, and you could not rightly call him a risk-taker by nature. He knew that he should not be visiting Ezhov's home, but he was curious to fathom a life-and-death issue that had come over our land. During one of our last meetings he leaned close to me and whispered: "Ezhov is only the agent." This had come after Babel had paid many visits to the Ezhovs and talked to Ezhov's wife, whom he had known for a long time. His were the only wise words I can recall from that whole period. Babel saw more than the rest of us and he made better sense of what he saw...

He was formed by the Revolution, and the fate of the man whom you now see before you (he indicated a large photograph on the stage of a smiling Babel) was a tragic one. Among Soviet authors, Babel was among the most committed to the Revolution. He believed in progress, in everything getting better.

And look, they murdered this man.

Had Babel survived and had he been without talent, his collected works would have been published ten times. I don't want you to think I am simply exaggerating for effect. I want us, as writers, to get involved and tell the publishers to print Babel; we also need to make sure that there are more evenings held in his honor...

I do not know what he was writing in his last years. He used to say that he was in search of simplicity. Babel's simplicity was not the kind that was being forced on us from above — it was simplicity rooted in complexity.

I must stress one thing. Babel was a major writer. And I say this not because I remain fond of him. To speak "objectively," as literary scholars like to say, Babel was the pride of Soviet literature.

I would like to see all of us writers working toward a common goal — that our countrymen be able to read Babel. It is said there is a paper shortage, but is there not enough to publish a single volume? We are not asking for endless volumes in a set of complete works. The paper simply has to be found.

I have been moved by all the speeches of those who knew Babel. I was also touched that they were being heard not just by those in the auditorium, but also by people in the corridors, the lobby, and even out on the street. I am happy for Babel, and I am happy that Antonina Nikolaevna and Babel's daughter, Lida, could both hear and see how fond people are of him.

Ehrenburg was warmly and frequently applauded both during and after his talk.

After the speeches, N. V. Penkov, an actor from the Moscow Art Theater, gave a wonderful reading of Babel's "My First Goose." Then Dmitri Nikolaevich Zhuravlev gave a brilliant reading of "The Beginning" and "Di Grasso."

Still, as well as things went that evening, neither the eightieth, nor the ninetieth anniversaries were celebrated by the Writers' Union. They were too frightened by the huge turnout for the seventieth anniversary.

✹

IN FEBRUARY 1967 my grandson Andrei was born and in the spring we needed to rent a dacha near Moscow. The Ehrenburgs wanted us to find a dacha near their own summer home in Novyi Yerusalim. I rented the lower floor (three rooms and a deck) from a professor's widow. I was already living on a pension, so I was able to spend the whole summer there.

We spent a great deal of time with the Ehrenburgs, and when I had to go into Moscow on business I usually drove back with them in their car.

One time I went over to their dacha, but Liubov

Mikhailovna was nowhere in sight, while Ilya Grigorevich was pounding away at his typewriter. I decided to sit on a couch out in the hallway until one or the other of them appeared. Suddenly the study door opened and a surprised Ehrenburg said to me, "Why didn't you just come in?"

"I didn't want to disturb you."

"Well, I was really hoping someone would — I really don't feel up to working just now."

On another occasion after we had finished our afternoon meal, Ehrenburg said, "Just imagine, Boris Polevoi had been trying to assure some foreign visitors of mine that we've been publishing Babel in millions of copies."

Lyubov Mikhailovna became very indignant. "When will they ever stop their lying?" to which Ehrenburg replied, "They've only just begun."

In June 1967 the French newspaper, *Le Monde*, ran a series of articles on Babel. Ehrenburg asked me over and spent over an hour translating the contents of the materials. These included Ehrenburg's own piece "A Revolutionary, But a Humanist," which I liked. His article ended, "Babel's death was premature, but he had done a great deal on behalf of our young Soviet literature. While he was a revolutionary, he remained a humanist. That was no small accomplishment."

Among the *Le Monde* articles on Babel was one by Pierre Dommergue in which he wrote about the influence of Babel's works on young American authors. He wrote that as far as style was concerned, American writers who once held Maupassant and Flaubert as supreme, were now turning to Artaud, Celine, and, above all, Babel. He mentioned American authors such as Bellow, Mailer, and Malamud, whose characters he saw as bearing a striking resemblance to Liutov in *Red Cavalry* — the same inability to adjust to violence; the same use of irony as a

Babel in 1938.

defense against the inevitable; "tenderness, cruelty, and lyricism: all of these expressed with humor and understatement" — these were features that Dommergue saw in both current American literature and Babel's writing.

Another article in the *Le Monde* series was by Petr Ravitch who wrote: "It is absurd to try to break a diamond down into its basic elements; the most one can do is to examine its spectrum. The same goes for the enormous talent of Isaac Babel." And he further stated: "By putting him to death at age 47 *(sic)*, this most Jewish of all Russian Jewish authors, a man who more than anyone since Gogol could make his readers laugh, having liquidated a member of the intelligentsia who was given to deep thought, yet adored horses and Cossack strength, the Soviet government committed an irreparable crime against Russian literature."

A third writer for *Le Monde* wrote that France had rediscovered Babel after Gallimard published his works. He added: "Just as the world can be reflected in a drop of water, so in one of Babel's short stories or even one of his brief phrases one can see reflected, as though through a well-focused magnifying glass, the world of the Bible, the Cossack epic, their traditions, another culture, the very inner essence of life in all its richness and variety. But the secret of his artistry lies in his sense of measure. And this artistry of his may be seen as a challenge to other writers: 'Try and say just as much, just as brilliantly, just as succinctly.' "

I was very grateful to Ehrenburg for translating these articles in detail, some of which I was able to record.

The summer of 1967 was the only time when I was able to stay in regular contact with Ehrenburg. Unfortunately, it was also the last time. That fall he died of a heart attack.

I always cherished everything connected with Babel. He was like a cult figure in our home throughout the years following his arrest. I surrounded myself with people who were close to him and regularly met with some women he had befriended in Odessa — Lidiya Moiseevna Varkovitska, whose husband had graduated from the Commercial Institute the same year as Babel; Olga Ilinichna Brodskaya, who had once been friends with Babel's sister. My closest friends were Isaac Leopoldovich Livshits, a schoolmate of Babel's, along with his wife, Liudmila Nikolaevna, and their daughter, Tanya.

I regularly corresponded and occasionally met with Tatiana Osipovna Stakh from Kiev; she and her husband, Boris, had been long-time friends of Babel, and their daughter, Sofia (Beba), had known Babel as a child.

Other constant friends were Yuri Karlovich Olesha, Nikolai Robertovich Erdman, Venyamin Naumovich Ryskind, and Semen Grigorevich Gekht. These were the only writers to ever pay visits to my "hopelessly tainted" home long before Babel was rehabilitated.

There were many people associated in some way with Babel whom I had not met while he was alive. After he was gone I wanted to meet them so I could talk about him.

My daughter, Lida, was the first to meet Babel's son, Misha. The poet Evtushenko had met Misha in the south and told him that he was acquainted with his half-sister, Lidiya *(sic)* Babel. Misha got Lida's telephone number and they arranged to meet. Lida told me that Misha was an artist who specialized in cityscapes of Moscow. One winter morning, looking out our apartment window facing Yauzskaya Street, I noticed a painter with his easel. I asked Lida to come see if it was Misha, and it was he. Lida went out to invite him in to get warm, have some lunch, and store his art supplies with us while he was working in the area. And that was how I came to meet Misha.

Misha showed me his birth certificate, brought me some photographs of Babel that had been left with him, and also brought me Babel's story "Sunset" after it was first published in *Literaturnaya Gazeta.*

I was very fond of Misha. He did not greatly resemble his father, but their bearing was similar, and he also had a number of physical traits that reminded me of Babel. We do not see each other very often, but he has a special place in my heart. He has become famous in Moscow for his cityscapes and has painted many spots in the city that no longer exist.

✻

I FIRST MET BABEL'S DAUGHTER Natasha in 1960. An exhibition of French paintings was being held in Moscow, and Natasha, together with her friend Tanya Paren, had come as interpreters. Both knew Russian and had been trained to work as art interpreters at exhibitions.

Natasha was about thirty, had finished the Sorbonne, and was teaching French literature in Paris. I found Natasha charming, jovial, and witty. To my mind at least she was my eldest daughter. She and Lida hit it off extremely well, and were willing to do anything for each other. Around this same time, Babel's sister, Meri, had come to visit us in Moscow, and she was amazed to see how close Lida and Natasha were becoming. She saw it as resulting from their being blood relations.

Babel's only Moscow relative was his Aunt Katya on his mother's side. She had married Iosif Moiseevich Lyakhetsky, and the two of them lived together with Lyakhetsky's brother and sister in an apartment on Ovchinnikovsky Lane. After Babel's arrest we were in constant contact with this family. Iosif Moiseevich died in the war, and after it was over, Katya's nephew, Mikhail Lvovich Poretsky, a war veteran, and his wife, Asya, moved in. Lida and I always looked upon these people as family and we were treated the same way in return.

Credit for the idea of collecting memoirs about Babel must be given to the Kharkov literary critic, Lev Yakovlevich Livshits. This was a fine young man who was completely consumed by his love of Babel's art. He turned up unexpectedly in Moscow during 1963 and paid me a visit. In 1964 he gave a paper on Babel at a conference entitled "Literature in Odessa of the 1920s," wrote several good articles on Babel, and was about to take up the theme of "Babel and the cinema." Everyone I introduced him to liked him, but then, while still a very young man, he suddenly died of a heart attack. This was a great loss, not just for those close to him, but for literature as well.

Livshits and I had only managed to prepare a preliminary list of people who could write memoirs about Babel. Now, it was up to me to continue the project on my own. I requested memoirs from his friends and acquaintances, and many of these obliged. Some reminiscenses had already been published in journals. G. N. Munblit and his wife, N. N. Yurgeneva, my official co-compiler, helped me to round up the various articles. Once these had all been collected and read, it became clear that I would also have to contribute in order to provide the fullest picture possible.

I wrote down whatever I remembered without any particular concern for chronological or thematic order. Once I had written everything down and reread it, I began to cut and organize the pieces. I saw that ordering the material chronologically would not work. I felt I should arrange it by following the line of Babel's encounters with different people all the way through his last meetings with them, and sometimes until the end of their lives. My memoirs were first published (with many deletions) in 1972 as part of a set of memoirs by contemporaries of Babel. The editors at Sovetski pisatel' Publishers were careful to expunge all the *criminal elements* from my text, as these were understood back then. For example, I was not even permitted to mention Babel's arrest. Other contributors were limted in the same way. While I was able to restore the deletions to the 1989 edition, many others died before it was possible to do so.

For the subsequent editions, I have added a few touches to Babel's portrait, some further material concerning his fate, and I have also written about my efforts related to the publication of his writings.

My major effort has gone into the preparation of the 1990 two-volume edition of his works. This included all his completed literary works, manuscripts that were left after his arrest, and everything that was published at least once during his lifetime. Consideration was even given to old manuscripts that had turned up. I began this work almost immediately after Babel's rehabilitation. The two-volume edition was meant to include all of the short stories from 1913 on, all the plays, scenarios, articles, letters, memoirs, speeches, and the 1920 Red Cavalry diary.

On many occasions the Babel Commission turned to the Writers' Union, first with the request to publish and then for assistance in getting the two-volume edition out. For many years we were told that there was no paper, and that the publication schedule had already been fixed, so that our request was carried over from one five-year-plan to the next. Finally, in 1986, twenty years after the last one-volume edition had appeared, the two-volume set was included in the publication plan for the

Khudozhestvennaia literatura Publishing House. The edition's run of 100,000 copies did not appear until January 1990.

Two other editions that I had prepared came out almost simultaneously: one was a supplement to the journal *Znamya*, and included the Red Cavalry diary; the other included Babel's best-known works and selected memoirs about him. Furthermore, without my participation, single-volume editions of Babel's books with modest press runs began appearing in many cities across the country. And so it has taken a full half-century after his death for the works of I.E. Babel — this writer so loved and respected throughout the world — to become available to a wide readership in his native land.

A NOTE ON THE AUTHOR

A. N. PIROZHKOVA was born in 1909 in
Siberia and had a successful career as a construction engineer, working for a time as a
designer on the Moscow subway project. In
1996 she left Russia to move to the United
States, and now resides in Maryland with her
daughter, Lida Babel, and her married grandson, Andrei Malaev-Babel.

❋

A NOTE ON THE BOOK

The text for this book was composed by
Steerforth Press using a digital version of
Walbaum, a typeface designed by Justus Erich
Walbaum in the early nineteenth century. The
book was printed on acid-free papers and
bound by Quebecor Printing ~ Book Press, Inc.
of North Brattleboro, Vermont.